Building a career in architecture

Joseph Healey

CONTENTS

PREFACE

- Personal introduction
- Why I have written this book
- My career path so far
- How this book is structured
- What you will get out of this book

Personal Introduction

I am a thirty-seven-year-old chartered architectural technologist. And from a brutally factual point of view, I am a failed architect. I began studying for an architecture degree in 2001, at the UK's highest rated built environment faculty, but for various reasons that you will find out, I did not complete the course and defaulted to Architecture Studies. 16 years, 7 companies, 3 continents, and numerous amazing projects later, I decided to write about my experiences and how, despite what can be a tough university experience, it really will not need to define your career. There are many avenues available to get involved in the industry, and there is no better time than now to jump into the subject and make it work for you.

I was born and brought up in Buckinghamshire in the middle of England. I attended the University of Nottingham from 2001 to 2005 and then spent eight fantastic years in a professional practice in London. Following a mixed year of travel and dream-chasing to work on the Rio de Janeiro Olympics venues, I then spent nearly five years in practice again in Abu Dhabi and Dubai, followed by a few months back in the UK, before relocating to my current home in Melbourne, Australia.

Why I have written this book

It was whilst supplying varied advice through architectural mentoring programmes over the years, and having to revisit my CV and portfolio several times, that I realised there was a lack of career-focused advice or basic industry literature for young architecture professionals.

Deeply theoretical and visual architecture books are plentiful, but to specifically read about early career years, understanding projects, fitting into the office atmosphere, and learning tough lessons, seemed to be an untold story. It is easy to find the huge glossy architectural books and glaze over the stunning global buildings that are so well known to whet your architectural appetite, but what about entry-level advice for architecture students and graduates trying to secure their first job? How can you make an impression once you secure employment? How do you go about forging a career path and setting yourself up for a rewarding journey ahead? All the best architectural theory, historical era textbooks, or complicated construction details are daunting and useless when you have got to simply perform your basic role in your first few years of work.

This book is intended partly as a career story, and partly as a learning and development aid for young or mid-career architectural professionals. It will be useful to school-aged students looking to build some architectural knowledge before aiming towards university, or useful to those beginning their architectural education or training. It may provide helpful guidance to architecture graduates in their first few years of practice, understanding the big wide world of work. There will also be some interest for people in later stages of their career, or anyone who just wants an insight into the industry. The book serves up real-life advice and practical tips for navigating this complicated but exciting road ahead. Even if you are career-changing into the profession, and need a rapid way to catch up on all that would otherwise be known by now, this book gives a good introduction of how things work and what to expect from day-to-day architectural life.

My career path so far

The scope of this book touches on my upbringing in the UK, followed by my university experiences at Nottingham, and all the lessons I learnt through those life-changing, formative years. My journey into professional practice started briefly in my hometown of Milton Keynes, then continued into London, thereafter to the Middle East, and finally to my current location in Melbourne.

In terms of roles, I have been an architectural assistant, a technologist, a project architect, a technical architect, a site architect, a technical coordinator, a senior architectural technologist, and finally, a specification writing expert. This book tells my story in the architectural industry so far, with the added intention of trying to prepare and encourage young architecture professionals to drive and shape their own careers, using this relevant and personal advice.

How this book is structured

The book is split into 3 sections. Firstly, a summary of the architectural industry in line with my experiences, and tips on understanding the basics. I have seen the good, the bad, and the ugly over my 16 years, both in buildings and in people. This first section features an overall view of construction projects; how the teams are arranged, the key phases and activities to be aware of, and how a vast number of different roles, skills, and personalities combine to produce beautiful and inspiring, or sometimes dysfunctional and heartbreakingly bad buildings. It also features some important lessons to learn and how to start

4

stitching together this long and winding road of your architectural career, potentially by pursuing further qualifications. It also includes which parts of architectural life I found to be most important in career development, some realistic CV and portfolio advice, and a quick summary of common building materials, just so you can appreciate the basics of building technology.

The second section has a kind of coffee-break structure, where you can dip in and out more easily. I have listed out my top 12 recommendations for career advice, and then how to gauge the personalities you will likely encounter in your own office as well as the wider project team. This is followed by a fascinating collection of external contributions, directly written by a wide variety of friends, colleagues, and contacts I have made over the years working in architecture. It is their take on the industry and what advice they would give to young professionals looking back on their career. Then an indulgent chance to describe some of my favourite buildings and why I like them, plus a few that I don't. Then follows a list of inspirational and meaningful quotes from famous architects, and then my own interpretation of what future advances and changes we might see in the industry over the next few decades. This section also features a handy architectural glossary, which lists some industry terms that I find are commonly misused or not easily understood. I hope you can browse through this second section to learn some common architectural terms, remind yourself of some interesting opinions, and to keep your architectural mind ticking.

The concluding third section is my career story thus far. It covers many architectural practice memories I can recall from my professional experience. Chronologically written, this also features real-life advice, stories, mistakes, lessons learnt, successes, failures, and my whirlwind story in this industry that I love to be part of.

What you will get out of this book

I certainly appreciate that the subject of architecture is too big to ever just pick up a book and fully educate yourself about, because there are so many subsets to focus on. It is a brilliant, amazing, enthralling subject, and in my opinion perhaps the most important in the world. There is so much to learn and that can often be pretty daunting. I have had my ups and downs over the years, so this account of a 'failed architect' shows that nearly 20 years after starting university, I am still living the architectural dream.

I hope this book will provide a trusted companion for real industry advice, tips, positivity, and experiences, but also warnings, frustrations, and dangers, taken from my career journey. I still enjoy active mentoring roles to this day and I hope this book can provide a written version of that advice. This book intends to at least provide useful information to stimulate your understanding, but also provoke debate and discussion, which is one of the most crucial aspects of living in the architectural world.

Finally, if you would like to connect with me or ask any questions about the book, perhaps tell me how useless it is, or argue over my like or dislike of certain buildings, I would be delighted to hear from you. This is just my story, and everyone else's is worth hearing too.

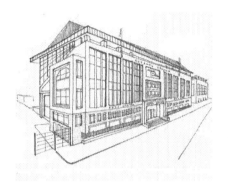

INTRODUCTION

i.   Studying architecture as a novice

If you are reading this book as an architectural novice, hopefully, the contents page will not frighten you off. There is far more to fear when you enter the industry than what is described in this book, but also far more to look forward to and embrace. Architecture always seemed like such a high-level subject to me when I was first considering my university choices, but I believe the subject really belongs to everyone. Even through tough times in my career when I might casually research other industries to see what level I could jump in at, the architecture industry still brings a huge amount of enjoyment, satisfaction, and education. The enthusiasm I have for building style, ingenuity, form, scale, and decoration is still as pleasing as it was many years ago and I think will always remain so.

There are endless reasons as to why architecture is an absolutely fascinating subject. It is ever changing and evolving, so there's always a new building to find out about and analyse. It is visually stunning but also interesting from the scientific and granular level. Architects are often controversial and challenge things, which can be fun to follow. Architecture as a subject represents both the history and future. Architecture directly shapes the planet we live on, and hopefully in my lifetime, it may define what we do on other planets too. Architecture is a place where you can exhibit your style in the most personal way, but also an opportunity to make a contribution to society to benefit everyone.

Whatever your level of understanding or involvement, architecture can be a really subjective profession. If you like arguing, architecture is good for you too. If you don't like arguing, you can stick with your own opinions on what you do and do not like. Hopefully, many more reasons will be gradually revealed to you in this book, not only from my viewpoint but from hearing about all the things that I witnessed along the way.

As a very general statement, I think architecture is a far more mainstream subject than it used to be when I was growing up in the 1990s. A complete beginner in the industry would normally require some good aptitude in mathematics, a basic understanding of physics, and a visual appreciation of good design. But even if you don't tick any of those boxes, but are simply interested and stimulated by the subject, now is a better time than ever before to give it a go, for the following reasons. Project sizes and project requirements seem to just keep expanding. The buildings, as well as the infrastructure to go with it, are getting bigger and bigger. There are more materials to deal with, more materials being invented, more regulations to adhere to, and therefore more liabilities that your company will have to be aware of. There are far more specialist roles too. The team structure and deliverables to be completed for a project are quite different to when I first started out. I feel like building typologies are more segregated now, so you will find expert designers in some building types who would consider themselves a complete novice in others.

The dilution of the traditional architect's role over the years has been noticeable and quite sad, because they have far less control than previously. That has been strangely helpful to other building experts who can still bring something very valuable to design and construction, without having the full architectural qualification. The traditional architect seems to be used more like a consultant now, just another expert who is at the mercy of contractor budgets and the fickle nature of their client's bank balance. Their input has been reduced and, in my opinion, is far less comprehensive than it used to be. Despite that, there are now so many distinct roles and requirements for building projects to be executed, that I am confident you will always be able to find a niche.

Architecture is a serious business, and takes a huge amount of people and their differing skills to make it all work. So, in that sense, if you are keen and learn the prevalent skills of the time, you will be hugely valuable and sought after. It might be more difficult towards your senior career years to find your niche because your billing rate (and therefore wage demands) are likely to be quite high, so companies need to find a way to get a lot of value out of you. Apologies if you consider yourself in this 'wiser' chapter of your career, everyone has their worth. Additionally, there are many more relevant qualifications available that can get you in the door now. Perhaps 30 years ago, you would have to be authentically and fully qualified as 'an architect' to make your way. But now, there are a huge number of routes in, where qualifications are potentially less specific, but all somewhat merge into each other in terms of applicable skills and flexibility. It all comes down to software skills now, so various qualifications can still lead to an architecturally orientated career, like engineering, graphic design, data expertise or BIM document management for example. Sadly, the credibility of your education is still quite dependent on the location and its reputation, so in my experience an architectural professional qualified from one country can have vastly different capabilities than another. The profession is one big melting pot of ideas, standards and abilities.

It seems that education from universities in Europe, North America and Australia are generally the most recognized for their credibility and knowledge, which can be painfully misleading. That is just one early lesson for how hard and unfair life can be, but your focus should be on the applicable abilities you possess, and how companies can use that in executing projects. It is always very much a business decision to hire staff. They want to employ you to do a job for the company, where they make money from your output. Don't ever forget that. Very broadly, that means 2 major things in terms of ability; BIM software skills, and understanding the construction of buildings. Then of course a quality you should possess in any career; a passion and feeling of worth in what you are doing.

ii.   My career overview

My involvement in architecture did not start particularly early. Growing up in the bizarre modernist concrete wonderland of Milton Keynes in the middle of the UK is an odd place to begin. But then visiting beautiful historical towns and cities around the UK in my teen years spiked some interest in architecture, despite also learning from drab, ugly, and stale places. Into my late teenage years, I did not have any direct experience of architecture and nobody in my family had either. Gradually, during college (aged 16—18 years), I realised that a design career could be my path forward. After a few summer weeks discussing my post-college options, I chose architecture, which seemed quite an exciting and important vocation.

After four years study at university, I was ready for

work. I spent several years in the amazing metropolis of London, featuring numerous European weekend trips, taking in all the diverse influences of capital cities, towns, and cultures. I then went further afield, spending three months in the astonishing south American country of Brazil, attempting to find work on the Olympics projects. After that brief unsuccessful spell, I found work in the Middle East, being surrounded and constantly wowed by the mind-bending but beautiful contradiction of hi-tech / Islamic architecture in Dubai and Abu Dhabi. After five years of employment there, I took a few months out for a career break, travelling to some interesting locations around the world; namely Cuba, South Africa, Botswana, Zimbabwe, the southern American states, followed by Girona and Greece. I relocated to Melbourne, Australia, in late 2019.

Looking back, I had no idea about architecture on day 1 of architecture school. But the fact that nineteen years later I am still hanging in there, means anyone with a passion and interest in how the world looks and functions can make a uniquely meaningful career in architecture: I failed two of the crucial modules during my 'Part 1' architecture degree, and eventually came out of university after one retaken year and one sidestep into an Architecture Studies honours degree. So, from that view, 'a failed architect' is a fair description of me. I was excited at the start of the course, but had become a bit exasperated by the middle of year 2, then had become completely drained in the middle of year 3, but lifted again by year 4. Luckily, that was a brief and ultimately, not too influential start of my career. You will soon realise that there is far more to be learnt from hands-on experiences, working on interesting projects, and diving into all that the industry can give back to you.

I am incredibly lucky to have travelled to so many places and been able to find work. Lucky also, that architecture is a fairly safe industry that has not advanced too much in terms of mass automation or obsolescence of the human touch. We always need buildings, so buildings always need designing, renovating, or replacing. That's the same anywhere around the world. Lots of people travel extensively in their profession and find themselves looking back on an amazing few years of employment in various locations, on exciting projects and with different companies. If that is your dream career path in architecture and construction, it is easily made into reality with hard work, a positive attitude, and an awareness of the skill sets you can offer.

My own roles and responsibilities have developed and changed several times in my career, as shown by my job titles. It has been so varied, and sometimes unexpected, which is probably the part I have loved most. The learning and developing experience from seeing so many unusual places, people, projects, and cultures have kept it exciting and interesting. The fact that the industry changes so much every week, means that there is always something new to learn about, and there's always an amazing architectural design you've never seen before. It is good to not know what is around the corner, but I now have enough skills and experience to feel like I could seek out a job nearly anywhere in the world.

iii.　What the book deals with

I wanted to take the time to look back on what has been a varied but hugely enjoyable career so far. I am very much in the mid-career territory now, so this book offers advice based on the experiences I have had. Some of these lessons you can take, some you will probably want to ignore or take the opposite approach, and some might be shocking, comforting, or amusing, but all true. Remembering where you have been, what you have done, how you got there and what you have learnt, is a valuable step at any time in life, let alone in your professional career.

Architecture is certainly an industry where real experience is vital and always unique to you. This book could be very similar in content to many other mid-career architecture professionals, but everyone's advice and interpretation of their career is valuably different, whether they had positive or negative experiences. Hence the importance of taking stock, being proud of what you have done, but making new targets and being excited about the road ahead.

You will meet all sorts of people in your career, and hopefully, work on many exciting projects, but it will be an epic ride especially if you treat it like that. Take every opportunity to 'talk-up' your career and projects. It is an exciting subject that can and should be a hobby, to bring you happiness and optimism. Particularly through my years mentoring in the UK, Middle East, and Australia, it has been great to see my views and experiences being interesting to others. I will reiterate several times in this book, this is just one architectural story, and everyone has fascinating tales to tell. I certainly find it hugely interesting to hear of others' career stories when they are excited and absorbed by them.

iv.   What the architecture industry is to me

There is nothing more depressing to me than someone who is really bored with their job, and does nothing about it. I can talk about architecture and the industry for hours. I genuinely enjoy it. Sometimes I can be talking about how frustrating it is, or how things do not go smoothly, but that is still with an edge of positivity that things can be changed and improved by the people who are directly involved in it. The subject is immeasurably valuable, and I love what human beings have been able to do with the built environment through engineering, mathematics, design, craftsmanship, philosophy, sociology, construction and rational thought and all that goes with basic human endeavour.

This is not to congratulate and celebrate the way we have developed the world in most recent years too much, because it is clear we are using resources at rapidly unsustainable speeds, but it is still fascinating to step back and analyse the position we have made for ourselves, and scrutinize how we use and develop planet earth. I am definitely a cynic, but would quickly say I am an optimist too, I love to debate and discuss the subject. I like to challenge the norm in search of efficiency and improvement. There is good reason why we don't live as we did in 1980, or 1950, or 1900, and it is all to do with human innovation and the innate urge to enhance what you have. Architecture can be the result of that feeling.

I have found over the years that there can sometimes be no better architectural education than going for a long walk, bike ride or bus journey to simply look around at the built environment. That's why I think it is a subject for everyone because we all share towns and cities, so everyone should be involved and have their say in it. The world should be a fair and democratic place where architecture serves the people, so that local values and cultures make a contribution to the success of a place. We need to protect that identity, and therefore protect why we are different, whilst learning about each other through subjects like art and architecture.

Countries and cities are all supposed to be so different due to their cultural setting, which makes travel and architecture such an exciting subject. But in some ways, I can see the world becoming, unfortunately, more repetitive in its metropolitan design. The fact that we move around the world so much now, sharing ideas, working in vastly different locations from where we grew up, causes problems. We subconsciously throw all our design knowledge together to end up with this global design style that is a little bit from everywhere, and hence a bit repetitive, whilst losing the cultural authenticity that we used to travel for. It is like a version of architectural globalization. The built environment is your backyard, and for the most part, people have some sort of affiliation and care for their backyard and what goes on there. So, you should really take care of the place you live too.

An enjoyable part of this book was to give my views on my favourite buildings through the years. This is not an academic appraisal in any way, and not a perfect theoretical assessment of the buildings to follow or agree with, but certainly a good description and viewpoint from a standard viewer like me. Architecture is an art form, and therefore, inherently an opinion. You design in the way your opinion believes it should be. It is a way of describing your values. An interpretation of your preference and style in a physical form. You could easily find more experienced and far more analytical assessments than mine, that could utterly contradict my analysis. However, I think you will find much of the regarded 'world's greatest architecture' might completely turn you off. You can visit famous artistic and architectural exhibitions, watch professional design TV programmes, learn from the winners of national and global architecture prizes, but your own opinion will rate some as beautifully innovative, and others as horrendous and confusing.

Whether people like a building or not, their reasons make the argument. Reasons give the intellect and the proof of opinions. But therein lies the beauty of the subject. Architecture is for everyone, and therefore, everyone has their voice, and thus, lots of people are likely to disagree. In my opinion, the act of discussion and debate is probably the most valuable contributor to the built environment, because we share and combine ideas and hopefully end up with the best of them. I would welcome a reply to any of my building descriptions. If by any chance you have been to them, spent time in them, or actually had a hand in designing or building them, it would be fantastic to hear from you and I would really value your thoughts on these buildings.

v.   Making a contribution in life

Maybe it's felt more in the architecture industry, but I think we are wired as humans to improve ourselves and to seek a way of achieving something. Even if that just means the instinct to get a job, earn money, and be in control of your surroundings in order to feel justified in life. Is an architectural career about feeling justified or worthy? Perhaps all jobs are a way of feeling that you are contributing to the world, but architecture is a more direct and more hands-on way of doing that. I need this job to feel like I am doing something in life for myself, my family, and for those around me. Justification and worthiness come out quite high in my personal reasoning. I like to think that the building designs I have been involved in over the years do make a dramatic difference to thousands of people each day. Is that just me, or the natural human endeavour to make an impact? I would be very glad if it is an inherent human endeavour and to feel like everyone has that drive. Overall, I think that is the essence of being in this profession. You care about its improvement and want to make positive contributions.

If I was not involved in architecture, I would be missing out. Just being able to visit, look at, and talk about buildings is good for the soul. I like browsing architecture websites every day, reading about new buildings and modern technologies, and knowing I had a hand in the creation of the places we live. I have gathered a good amount of knowledge and have organised my favoured design styles above others, so to execute a personal design at some point would be the ultimate goal. Maybe by the time I write book number 2, it will be a self-help book for building your own dream house.

Key points:

*   The industry has diversified and it is much easier to approach than previously.

*   Early years revolves around your software skills.

*   Architecture can be your job, and your hobby.

SECTION 1 – ARCHITECTURE IN PRACTICE

1.1   UNDERSTANDING PROJECTS

1.2   BUILDING YOUR CAREER IN ARCHITECTURE

1.3   CURRENT INDUSTRY SKILLS

1.4   COMMON BUILDING MATERIALS

1.5   QUALIFICATIONS POST GRADUATION

1.1   UNDERSTANDING PROJECTS

1.1.1 The basics of architecture and building.

1.1.2 How projects are executed.

1.1.3 Billing rates, contracts, project stages.

1.1.4 Attending meetings, project communication.

1.1.5 Drawings 'where', schedules 'what', specs 'how'.

1.1.6 Seeing the design process evolve.

1.1.7 A summary of project roles.

1.1.1 The basics of architecture and building.

After a few years in any industry, it is good to come back to your roots and remind yourself of the basics. I have plenty of years behind me now, and the industry has changed so much since I started, but I still find it useful to stand back from my daily tasks and read about construction projects, have a look at building sites as I walk past, study detailed drawings from online magazines, visit great buildings in person, and just enjoy the subject for what it is. It is essentially just designing, drawing, and constructing buildings for people to use. In the same way that anything in the world is designed for a purpose, for example, cars, chairs, clothing, or simply a pencil; architecture is creating something for humans to use that makes their life easier, or more enjoyable. For the most part, architecture is serving the public.

So, on that note, what is an architect? Where are the boundaries of their responsibility? Who are the other professionals involved in construction, like builders, developers, surveyors, architectural technologists, interior designers, and engineers? What is the architecture profession really like, and how can you be involved in this huge subject?

In this section of the book, I will discuss in quite general terms, how the architecture profession operates in terms of designing and constructing a building. Who does what, who is managing who, how projects are executed, and how everyone involved overlaps along the way. Understanding architectural projects fully requires more education and understanding than I could ever describe in a few paragraphs and more than just this book. But hopefully, in the early stages of your career, you can use this information as a good platform to start from.

Like many jobs, learning from the bottom first gives you a perfect appreciation of the most basic skills needed, and what a huge subject this is. After a few years of experience, the same frustrations, or the same cycles of work can become a little monotonous. Looking back on the past can really help visualize your future, in terms of understanding change and seeing the industry patterns to allow you to prepare. Reminding yourself of where your enjoyment and development peaked in the past, can be helpful to know your future direction.

Once you have been directly involved in projects for around ten years or more, you will have broad experience and knowledge. However, there will always be more to learn, because the continuous search for innovation and efficiency in modern design and construction, will supply new and exciting topics to keep you on your toes. Technology is so widely adopted along the entire project timeline now, and it is presenting so many better ways to design and execute projects. You need to be well aware of industry changes to avoid getting left behind.

The changing definition of an architect

An architect, by definition of the word, is a 'Chief-Builder.' So, perhaps that definition pushes towards all-encompassing building knowledge, as opposed to just the design and construction of buildings. The modern interpretation of an architect has become vastly different from the chief builder, with many subsets and deferred roles compared to the original version. A good example is my professional qualification, being a Chartered Architectural Technologist, which has still allowed me to spend all these years in the industry in several roles, without being fully qualified as a UK registered architect.

I see architecture as one of the world's oldest professions because, at its most basic level, humans have always needed shelter. Shelter is fundamentally a form of protection from the weather and the environment, which is effectively a building. Initially, caves were used for shelter and protection, but over thousands of years, we have arrived at this point of man-made protection, which goes way beyond that initial rationale of shelter. It is one of the most basic needs of human beings and animals. We are all here to survive and thrive, and cannot do that without our modern version of architecture.

Once you have shelter, you will probably want to improve it, then expand it, then make it better, and so the design process and endeavour begins. Historically, there has always been a blend between architecture, engineering, craftsmen, artists, and masons. Now, we have so many specialist roles within building projects that you can divide up the industry into many different responsibilities, all broadly originating from those above. Each discipline has many sub-sectors below it, which you will see for real in your projects and your team members' job titles. However, their common skill is knowledge of buildings and their components. Therefore, the science behind materials, structures, and of course, good functional design is the key.

Science, art and technology

Do you consider architecture to be a science or an art? Perhaps it's now become more of a combination of the two. During my architecture education, it was commonly classed as an Art, for example, the traditional qualification is a Bachelor of Arts (BA Hons) in Architecture. But the technological influence in the world has brought science into that reasoning. This also blends into physics and an increasing use of biology in architecture (biophilic design), by understanding nature's structures and laws to give a basis for our own buildings. Many of the buildings built today would simply not be possible without extensive science and technology expertise and application.

An architect's role has changed vastly in the last 20 years, and their pertinent skills have become blended with the developing role of architectural technicians or technologists. In my experience, their knowledge and skill levels are very similar, but project architects are more in tune with the day to day running of the project and client relationships. Increasingly, that means more administration or organisational tasks as opposed to the details and drawings.

There are many ways to be involved in the design and construction of buildings, and hence many avenues to utilise your skills and knowledge. In that sense, the subject has become more mainstream too, where architecture has opened up as a subject, to be viewed more as a public owned representation of how towns and cities should serve their people. It needs the fresh new influence of young people too. Humans are constantly changing; hence buildings and places need to change with them to keep serving our needs and improving our lives. Particularly in my recent few years, I have found a lot of pride in understanding that in architecture, you are contributing to better-designed places, and consequently, better use of those places, therefore, a happier society.

The need for projects

Being involved in architecture can take many forms, but my experiences concern professional practice and building projects. The basic concept is that a person or company wants to build or refurbish a building, so they need to engage and pay several specialists to do that, and they intend to make money from that building. Public buildings broadly have the same first two concepts, without necessarily wanting to make money in the same way if they are government buildings for example, but for most of your career, you will see that property, and therefore architecture, is increasingly dominated by money and ownership of assets. Every penny is scrutinised much more than ever, and the sums of money involved in investment and property development seem to be at an all-time high. The finance of development is a whole separate subject to get involved in if you want to, but my experiences here stick to working for architecture companies, designing buildings, and being involved in their construction and eventual occupation.

Why do we do it this way

You will find different approaches all around the world, but I find it interesting to grasp that the current method the way it is now, is a result of all that has gone before it. It will continue to change in the future, but if you think in most simplistic terms, the way projects are run now is exactly down to the methods and attitudes of the people involved, and the governmental or commercial frameworks that they are surrounded by. At any point in time, the industry was moving along just fine and constructing buildings, until a new approach or strategy was suggested, and so the industry changed a little to adopt it. Then other improvements were made for efficiency or cost reasons, so companies reacted and adopted that too. Over the course of many years, changes, improvements, and innovations were made and adopted to lead us to our current status. We are a product of what has gone before.

Trying to consider how the world's oldest buildings were designed and erected is very difficult but fascinating. There were no large printers to show the design, no online models, and no huge cranes, or GPS to organise building sites. Was it just precision, communication, and dedicated workmanship that created places like the Acropolis, or the Pyramids, or the Colosseum? A few decades ago, without email or quick messaging, projects were executed mostly via phone calls, personal visits, and mostly 2D drawings sent in large parcels by post. That seems ridiculous now. To execute projects in 2021, we have amazing 3D visualizations, multiple skill sets for each discipline, hugely intricate data records to help us design, check, and plan out each stage, with changes made by the second, for the whole design team to see.

What I am trying to demonstrate, is that projects are run in the current way, because of our own evolution of how best to do it. Nobody is telling the construction industry how to improve, develop, or refine their techniques. As a collective industry, we are all trying to find the best ways to design and construct buildings. We are evolving our own preferences, so whichever methods are being used now, they are by default the current best way to do what we want to do. A classic British phrase is that 'the proof is in the pudding.' So, until something better comes along, the state of the architecture and construction industry is exactly down to those who work in it. Innovation becomes such a crucial aspect of architecture to move it forward.

Key points:

• Architecture as an art or science, or maybe both, is now hugely technological.

• Fundamentally, architecture is simply designing and constructing buildings for people to use.

• Architecture is a huge subject that you can't shortcut, so find a niche.

• The industry right now is a snapshot of the current best practice; it will soon change.

1.1.2 How projects are executed

Learning about project execution in terms of hierarchies, responsibility, and liability, with all the associated contractual understanding between companies, is really a big deal. There is a lot to understand. Delivering projects from the organizational and contractual side, sometimes known as project execution, is separated from daily drawing, modelling, coordination, and detailing. To actually run an architectural project is more about payment schedules, target dates, resources, deliverables, statutory requirements, information exchange, and of course, money. Whole books as thick as a door have been written about building projects and how to execute them, so there is a long road ahead to learn that, which will only come with experience. There are so many other facets to absorb, like contracts, legal duties, construction programmes, insurance, administration, building site logistics, and all the small nuances of how those work together. They are all specialist subjects in themselves, so I will touch on them where necessary. Here I will give a quick overview of how the majority of my 'design and build' projects were run, to give you a representative summary to start with.

Risk and liability

Projects are so much more than just the drawings you produce. Architecture and construction are massive, global, influential industries. They are often financially driven, and therefore, very contractually driven too. A massive part of the industry is about risk and submitting your project documents without getting sued for them at some point. Relevant terminology to find out more here would be terms like construction law, construction litigation, construction contracts, project management, construction liability, construction documentation, and the RIBA Plan of Work is particularly useful for overall project stages. That should keep you going for plenty of hours of study, and spin-off into all sorts of questions and curiosities about the legal world of architecture.

A huge point of understanding to pause on here, is liability. You might often hear, when someone has fully qualified as an architect, that they will be congratulated with the words "well done, you can now get sued." It is a humorous greeting to the grim reality that, as a registered practicing architect or architecture professional, your designs, decisions, and choices will directly affect the safety and functionality of buildings and their users, for years to come. Therefore, if you are proven to have omitted, forgotten, incorrectly designed, or specified something erroneously, you or your company can get penalised for it. It is a sobering thought when you have just put years into studying, but also crucial to know in the grand scheme of things, liability is probably the biggest issue that underpins the whole industry. In the same way that the world seems to be driven by money much of the time, the architecture industry is, unfortunately, no different, but we will try to stick to the pure architectural principles here instead of diving into the financial side.

Luckily, the management, contractual and financial aspects of projects are not really going to be at the forefront of your career development early on, but it will be helpful to keep absorbing that information, and at least understand how the pieces are moving. For my following examples, I will discuss projects from the viewpoint you will have in your first few years in practice. Your main roles will be drawings, modelling, coordination, and detailing, so I will stick mostly with those responsibilities, which links in with the patterns of projects that you will most likely be exposed to. Who does what, why, when, and how? Appreciating each company's overall duties, responsibilities, and intentions in the project can be a great way to learn, and show you how to behave.

The main players of a construction project

In some of my project experience, I was peripheral to the project running, whereas in others I was attending most of the meetings, handling all my team's drawing submissions, controlling the consultant's design and submissions, and staying connected with client developments for the direction that the project was going. They were equally enjoyable for different reasons, but I definitely learnt more when I was thrown in at the deep end with a good project director looking over my shoulder. There should always be someone more experienced to ask questions of, which should build your confidence too. Here I want to outline the most important parts of projects that you should understand in your early years, which I find always works well with an analogy. In this case, perhaps designing and building a house for a close friend.

There are many companies involved at different levels, all trying to operate as a business, and therefore, make money (or at least avoid making a loss on a project). For most of this section, it is important to understand that details can be vastly different in each project, so a deeper overall industry understanding will have to come with time, and ideally, you will see all stages actually happening within your project. But you must always think of the bigger picture, by that I mean each person and each company is involved in their own way, making their own large or small contribution, so it is good to understand how.

Concerning the house-building analogy, the bottom line is, there is a need for this building. Either as a house to live in, or to make money from it being rented out, or to eventually sell it for more than it cost to build. So fundamentally, your friend needs a house design, and then someone to build it. A diagrammatic representation is crucial to picture this, showing the client (your friend), the contractor, designer, consultants, specialists, suppliers, and of course legal / official bodies.

The project hierarchy describes the order of importance and influence in which each company operates. That basically comes down to who is paying who for their services, and who is telling who what to do. The project fundamentally starts with the client (or developer) asking an architect to produce a design for their plot of land that they own or to improve their existing building. This is known as the brief. It should outline the main requirements of the project in terms of size, style, timescale, and possibly the materials to be incorporated. The client's brief usually gives lots of accurate parameters, but can sometimes be loose and vague too. It is the architect's and design team's job to interpret it correctly and produce a design that satisfies it, which your client friend also likes architecturally. Other specialists within the design team (usually called consultants), will be employed by the architect at certain times, but the most common of those is the structural engineer and mechanical engineer, who will be involved to interpret the brief with the architect and produce workable, conceptual designs.

Over these first few weeks or months, various design skills and construction knowledge are combining, but it is mostly the architect who understands and controls the overall project concept, and organises the drawings. For this reason, the architect company is often called the 'Lead Consultant.' In simple terms, they are the first point of contact for the client during the design phase and 'lead' all the other consultants (structural engineer, mechanical engineer, plumbing and electrics engineer, landscape architect, sustainability consultant, and sometimes other specialists) in terms of coordinating and finalising the design. They are usually employed directly by the

31

architect, hence paid by the architect, and their skills are needed in order to complete the design as it moves towards a buildable set of drawings. Subcontractors are generally the suppliers of actual building products but can be directly employed by the consultants as required. This could be for packages like the cladding, internal doors, windows, or sanitary fittings. Every project will be slightly different in this sense, so it is definitely advisable to check in with your project director quite frequently and ask for some current project diagrams, responsibility matrices, or consultant information.

It may help you to see the project team demonstrated in a diagram, as below. The slight difficulty being that arrangements could be different depending on your project set up, and upon searching online for construction project diagrams, there are endless contradictory results. However, to keep it fairly simple, this shows the typical company relationships in terms of hierarchy, that you can discuss with your project director.

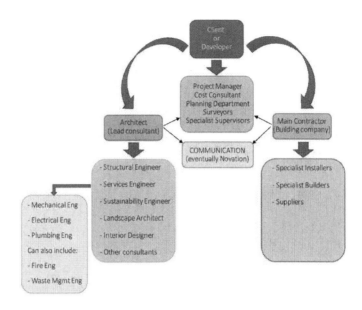

The various regulations and permissions the project must adhere to can be slightly different depending on location, typology of the building, and how sensitive it is to the local authority. Once your design team's various drawings show the project accurately, you can request planning permission, whereby the local authority will want to understand how it looks, what impact it has on the local area and what the construction disruption will be. Planning permissions is a massive hurdle to get over, and operates very differently in different countries, or particularly sensitive locations. It is worth a chat with your project director to discuss their recent experiences of planning permission, ideally for your current project.

The planning authorities

Think in terms of the neighbourhood you live in, or the

area where you work, or what the town centre is like. Different areas of the town or city have certain types of buildings. There is a good reason why a huge shining skyscraper full of businesses and financial institutions are generally not built in small, quiet residential streets where families live. A house building company would not build a huge residential development right next to a landfill site or sewerage works, because of the smell, and you would not want a zoo or park right next to an airport or next to noisy manufacturing plants. The built environment is generally planned out and organized so that the pattern of life is beneficial for the people who live there and society as a whole.

Take a look on Google earth at a town you know well, and see how areas of warehouses and industry are generally all clumped together. Retail or shopping precincts are concentrated to allow a better shopping experience for the people, and therefore better sales for the shops. You might notice that the city or town usually has a nice big park in the centre, often near a river or lake, with housing just outside of the core, instead of right in the middle. There's probably a train station fairly central, with hospitals and schools spread around but very accessible too. The cafés and restaurants are mostly in the middle, whilst airports would mostly be on the periphery. There is a good reason for all that planning of land.

Planning authorities decide not only what can be built where, but also what type of building is permitted, in terms of typology, density, potential knock-on effects of that building, and overall architectural style of the area. Many areas in the world are heritage listed, so ultra-modern buildings would not be permitted there. The ratios and combinations of industrial, commercial, agricultural, residential, cultural, community, retail, parkland, entertainment, transport, healthcare, power plants, or government buildings all need to fit together and work for overall benefit. Planning a town is crucial to organise what goes where, to allow business to flourish, people to move around the place and use the facilities, and therefore, to create a productive society.

Getting started on the project

So, back to the house build. The initial design simply shows what you are going to build, what it is going to look like, and how it will affect the local area or streetscape. Building regulations are the guidance and frameworks for how to correctly design buildings, and each country around the world usually has official government-held regulations or standards to ensure a good level of building quality for anything being constructed. You will usually need verification and approval from the council in order to start any project. Occasionally, planning permission will come with some 'conditions,' like small changes to your design, or guarantees that need to be demonstrated before you finally get permission to begin digging in the ground.

The next step is that a building company (the main contractor) looks at your drawings and can agree to an overall contract with the client (your friend), to build the project. The main contractor should have a pretty clear idea of all the costs, time, and materials required for this building from their experience or studying all your documentation like schedules, drawings, and specifications, which we will come to shortly. By interrogating your drawings and the consultant drawings, then often setting out a list of uncertainties or questions that they would like answers for, they quote an overall cost to build the house. You will hear a lot about 'tender' drawings as quite a major milestone or 'line-in-the-sand' for executing projects. This is because your drawings may have started as a simple sketch, elevation or basic view of a detail, but they will need to develop and improve to a point where they can be accurately used for tender. That means the whole project can be 'priced' from these drawings, by the main contractor (or their quantity surveyor). There can and will be changes after the tender drawings' submission, that will be recorded and dealt with in different ways, but tender is a point at which costs can be fairly accurately judged and agreed upon. Hence, your friend will have been given this price by the main contractor and can decide that yes, they would like to go ahead with the build at that cost, or maybe they would like to look at reducing the costs or even adding some extra features to the design. In simple terms, this would be like booking a holiday where for example, you want to know pretty accurately the total costs for the flights, hotel, activities, food, entertainment, etc., whilst accepting there might be some slight variance when you are there.

As I mentioned, it's impossible to wrap up the workings of all projects in one quick paragraph, so it's important to find the facts of your project and chat them through with the project leader, because it may differ slightly from the above.

Just about every part of the building should be shown on your drawings at this stage because if not, the main contractor will say that nothing was declared on the tender drawings, and therefore, they could build what is easiest and cheapest. All the materials, products, fixings, finishes, accessories, and building standards being adhered to should be quantifiable, hence the job of a quantity surveyor. Later in the project, if there is a dispute about the construction or finer details, the main contractor would be able to say that they are building 'in accordance with the tender drawings.' Your tender drawings were a line in the sand to establish what the main contractor must produce. Hence if you have not shown something on the tender set of drawings, it has not been declared, therefore, has not been priced, so you might need a 'variation' to make any changes. That's another term I will come to shortly, which is worth a few minutes of further study to get your head around.

The main contractor can now prepare the site in various ways; start earthmoving, hiring their building equipment or workers, ordering cranes, coordinating underground sewer connections, arranging the foundations around them, ensuring any existing electric cables or pipeline connections are known and can be worked around. There is a lot to be organised. Site boundary walls around the plot will also be erected so that it is officially designated and protected as an official working site. As I will come to later, any chance you get to look at building sites is a great way to learn, because the reality of construction is very detached from working in an office.

So now the project is effectively in the hands of the main contractor. They have your drawings and all the permissions they need, so they should be able to go ahead and build the project accurately for your friend. The tender drawing set is gradually developed and updated to be the 'construction set' (and eventually the 'As-Built' set), but these divisions of project phases will be set out in the contract more accurately. On paper, it should be fairly clear what should happen when, what it will cost, and how it is going to be done. However, there are very few projects that have ever gone completely smoothly in terms of building what was originally drawn. There will always be little changes, and always be uncertainties moving forward, but sometimes these develop further into arguments and disagreements, which delays work. And that leads nicely, as I mentioned, into variations.

Variations and changes

Another whole book can probably be written about how variations affect projects, but basically, once you have agreed on the cost of the build and the main contractor has accepted all your drawings, anyone working on the project might reasonably want to make a change or improvement. It could be small, easily adopted, cheap to implement, advantageous for the project, and everyone might be happy with it. But most likely, because this small change might affect a few other things too, it needs to be officially called a 'variation.'

This is essentially because there's money and liability involved. A variation can be raised by the main contractor, the architect, or the client. Perhaps your client wants a better quality of floor tiles, or wants the bathroom made slightly bigger. Conversely, the main contractor might reveal that something has not quite been built as drawn, or a slightly different product needs to be used because the original is not available. Usually, this request will be for the better of the project, or just to benefit one particular company who raises it. But if there is any slight delay of time, a slight increase in cost, or a slight difference to what was initially agreed, one of the companies may want compensation and will demonstrate how it negatively affected their company's costs. This basically comes down to money, because it can have a knock-on effect on a company in terms of time, materials, and resources spent.

As with those holiday plans I mentioned, you might have the flight, destination, hotel, and activities planned, but if one of your friends suddenly wants a different flight, or a slightly different hotel, or some extra activities included, or they are desperate to go to certain restaurants, you would have to put some effort into making these amendments or cancelling bookings, which may cost you. It can be done, but there is disruption and potentially extra money to pay, which affects the smooth running of this trip. From an official capacity on projects, you would usually track who has made which variation, why they did it, and what the knock-on impacts are. It is effectively a blame game and can get very messy and tense, but companies have to protect themselves from this risk and keep close records of it all.

To study variations from the client's side, think of the project as ordering a large cake for your birthday. So, you are the client, and you want an amazing cake for the big day. First of all, decide what flavours you want, what it will look like, as well as the size and shape. From this 'design' side of things, you might have a fair idea of how it will be done or where to get the ingredients, but it is not your problem because you hire a friend to make it. They are now the main contractor. Because of your specific preferences for this special cake, it must be the exact ingredients from the exact suppliers. Your friend must then know when it is all going to be delivered in order to start baking.

You want the cake to have 3 levels of sponge, with raspberry jam between one layer, apple jam between the other, topped with icing sugar, and decorations on top. It also needs to be ready on the morning of your birthday. So, the 'brief' should be pretty clear to the friend who is making it. With the best of intentions, like any project, some of this might go slightly wrong, but it is reasonable to expect that your birthday cake should be exactly as you have requested. The sequencing of ingredients arriving to your friend's house is crucial, just like when different building products arrive on site. They will have to figure out where they can temporarily be stored before needing them, or in this case, ensuring there is enough fridge or cupboard space to adequately store the ingredients before they are needed. Timing is crucial.

However, inevitably, problems arise. Perhaps the supermarket does not have enough icing sugar, so your friend cannot cover the whole cake with icing as requested. That will go down as a variation. They could frantically search for another supplier, or try to make do with only covering the top. But you have made an agreement about how it should look, so instantly you would feel like you are not getting what was ordered. Should the overall cost now be reduced? However, as the client, you might say it is no big issue and the icing can cover the top. Separately, the apple supplier says they cannot deliver until the next day, which is going to compromise the filling layer. So there will be a substitute for standard supermarket apples. That's a variation. Perhaps the candles supplier gets delayed delivering the day before the party, so your contractor friend must quickly source some candles from a local shop. Maybe not the exact candles you specified, but for visual purposes, they are the same. Would that be okay? You might let it go, but that's a variation to the final product too. The fundamental point for all these changes is, have you got what was agreed and costed for? Has the quality of the final product been affected?

The legal position of each company

Unfortunately, like much of life, it all comes down to money. From one point of view, you have agreed to something and have got 90% of what you wanted; had a great day, so let's all move on. But rarely in the building industry is it that simple. For the most part, companies will have pretty tight contractual agreements in place that will say, 'sorry but you owe me money for that mistake,' and for all the other small mistakes that were recorded over the project. There can be many months, or sometimes years of dispute, to decide who owes what sum for which mistakes, often way after the building is actually complete.

Main contractors, architects, and engineers are suing each other all the time, but then the resolution sometimes comes down to how willing each company is to hire legal teams and fight for financial compensation. Do you want to meticulously investigate every single drawing or detail to see who is wrong, and spend time, money and resources on this argument? Legal cases will dig out historical company emails, pinpoint phone call discussions, scrutinize schedules and approvals, find out whether companies acted in a timely manner, and basically build a case as to why a certain company is to blame. Often millions of pounds or dollars are at stake, not to mention professional reputations and ongoing business relationships for future projects, so it might be necessary to chase this resolution for the sake of the company balance sheet. It is a tough balance but works in the same way as personal disputes.

Perhaps think of it as a disagreement with your neighbour, about a broken fence that your properties share. How did it get damaged? Was it anyone's fault? Could you just fix it yourself in about 20 minutes and move on? But is it going to be expensive to do that? Are your neighbours refusing to help, even though it is partly their fence too? Can you arrange to share the cost? Or do you want to push them to rectify it fully at their cost? But that is going to negatively affect your neighbourly relationship. Do you want the other neighbours in the street to know you are arguing? Then do you really want all the hassle of going to court and seeking the lawyers to make the call for you, by which time you will probably never want to speak to this neighbour ever again? Maybe that's all too much hassle and you can settle this between yourselves in a reasonable manner, and keep your good friendship going. After all, you never know when you might need your neighbours' help with similar issues in future.

Different routes out of these disputes are often taken, which again, all comes down to money. What are the costs vs benefits of all these disputes, and what is best for the company to move forward? These must be considered. If this part of project liability and legal action excites you, look up terms like litigation, construction lawsuit cases, and construction arbitration.

Relationships during the build

To take a step back in the project, once the main contractor is engaged, there will be a huge learning curve as the project moves towards starting on site. You might hear the term 'novation,' which is when the design work is broadly completed, but the architect's responsibility and reporting transfers from the client, to the main contractor. If they have a 'design and build' (also called design and construct) contract, the architect works closely with the contractor from this stage onwards, to discuss and monitor finer design issues and find where improvements can be made. The main contractor gets more influence over the design after novation, hence trying to replace certain products or systems with cheaper alternatives, but the architect is still involved to protect the design quality. All parties need to be happy with the proposals, but if the same building objects can be procured for less money, it can be argued to be a good option for the client and main contractor. A process of 'value engineering' is often used to trim down costs for any part of the project, typically involving the cost consultant, architect, and contractor.

Instead of trying to describe all this in too much detail, especially at a point where you don't need to know the ins and outs, talk to your project architect, and undertake some light reading about 'design and build' versus 'traditional' contracts.

Involvement through the construction phase

Back to our house building example. As an architectural professional, you still have a considerable influence on the result whilst the build is happening. Ensuring the client is getting an accurate version of the building that you have designed for them, and keeping relations friendly during that process, can be quite a skill. You will hear phrases like 'managing expectations' and 'client relationships' used a lot. The architect's role is to anticipate improvements or raise possible flaws, which you can try to encourage your client to adopt and pay for. You will be visiting the site to witness installations, make site reports, watch on-site testing, give approvals or check samples, and take plenty of photos to document how the main contractor is performing.

In a good example that I can remember from a historical refurbishment I worked on in London, the main contractor and site manager were surprised to find crumbling brickwork behind some old plasterboard that they had removed as part of the renovation. My tender drawings clearly stated to retain, patch up, and repair any original damaged brickwork, and not under any circumstances, reduce the floor space unless verified by the client. However, the main contractor was adamant that the brickwork was not safe, and wanted to introduce a large steel column and cover that with plasterboard. The drawings categorically stated the approach, the structural engineer had agreed the brick was safe, and the main contractor had signed up to this by accepting the tender drawings. So, I stood my ground and had to watch him become quite frustrated at having to organise the repair, but the correct documentation of the tender drawings was my big saviour. I was acting in the best interests of the client, to keep this valuable and historical brickwork, whilst the main contractor did not care much about heritage and wanted to take the easy option by removing it all and covering it up.

It is the solving of problems there and then on-site which can be exhilarating and educational. Often quick hand sketches done hastily on-site need to turn pretty quickly into documented drawings, and integrated into the actual build, at late notice. Each discipline within a project will have a certain reputation, so you will gradually start to hear the stereotypical attitudes amongst project colleagues. As mentioned, each company is trying to operate for their own benefit, sometimes to the detriment of others, but working for an architect means you value quality and good design, even when it means extra cost or effort.

Talk to your project team or project runner about where each company sits within the project diagram. Hopefully, within your company project files, there ought to be diagrams to describe which companies are responsible for which design submissions. It should feature very useful information about how the project is going to be run, and which companies you talk to directly or via alternative channels. The communication around the design team needs to be quite strictly organised.

Completing construction and the tactics involved

Once the building work is nearly complete, getting to the handover stage is really fun and educational. Understanding the politics is great because at this 'snagging' stage the project is probably 90 / 95% done, but that last little effort should ensure a final touch of quality to achieve 'practical completion' for your client. However, you are back to the original three companies pulling in three different directions, and they all have differing intentions.

A 'snagging' or 'defects' list is usually compiled by the architect. It is a spreadsheet or chart to record all the small improvements, repairs, and rectifications that need completing, on any part of the construction that is not quite right. The architect often walks around the nearly completed building with the client to formulate this list. Once agreed, it passes to the main contractor to remedy these final issues, so that practical completion can be agreed upon where, as suggested, the project is more or less complete and the client will be able to start using the building.

So, concerning the three companies, and speaking very generally, the main contractor's view and duty is to get the build finished exactly as agreed upon. They are almost washing their hands of this job to move onto their next one, and ideally with some profit made from how quickly or efficiently they completed the work. In my experience, they might be a little bit resistant, because then you and your client friend are effectively hassling them for this final little effort, which to them, seems quite picky and fussy. They might say changes or requests are too late and their staff have moved on, but they also know the importance of remaining agreeable and fair in order to ensure a satisfied client and architect, for a good chance of future work. So, unless they want to create a potential argument, the main contractor will carry out these snagging tasks.

Secondly, your friend; the client. Their building project is nearly finished, so in one sense they are (hopefully) very happy and positive that it is nearly done, but they should also be pushing you and the main contractor to fulfil their obligations, tidy up all the loose ends and ensure quality. They might accept the specialist advice from either you or the main contractor if something can or cannot be done to achieve a better final building, or they might insist that things must be completed exactly as shown on the drawings and snagging report.

Thirdly, from the architects side you are hoping to

move on to the next job, trying to sign off in the best possible way. That final bit of quality is important for your own company reputation, for website photos, and marketing literature, but you do not want to spend too much time on this phase because the fees are typically quite low. The design phase provides the majority of their fee, whilst the construction, completion, and final handover is far less. You might be able to jump in and volunteer for the snagging job because your director will want to send a relatively junior member of staff to compile snagging lists. Another consideration is that your client might have more jobs in the pipeline, so you must remain loyal and thorough, to potentially have another project to be employed for.

Finally, the stage of handover can take place whereby the client officially has control of the building and your actions just about stop, apart from checking back for the 'in-use' phase. There should be a commissioning and feedback framework in place, to analyse and measure how effective some of the design decisions were, like the efficiency of the PV panels, green roof usage, or energy savings. Like any big event or project that comes to an end, hopefully, relationships have survived and the positivity from completion contributes to a successful ongoing partnership, whereby the companies will combine again for more projects. So, in that sense, it is crucial for each company to be putting enough resources into this phase and achieve a good send-off, but not spending too much time where things drag on. It all becomes quite tactical.

Key points:

- Drawings are just one part of project delivery.

- Liability, contracts, and money are still the fundamental factors of construction.

- Each company has slightly different priorities, intentions and motivations for the project.

- Variations and resolution of disputes have a major bearing on project success.

1.1.3 Billing rates, contracts, project stages

To correctly understand project costs and budgets is another big and separate subject. When I started in practice, an architect's project fee was looking at around 5% of the total construction cost of the building, but that has vastly changed. Hence their fee getting pinched more and more. The innovative influence of structural and mechanical work that engineers have to do has increased their value. The engineering fees can often be higher than the architects. Fundamentally, each company is obviously trying to cover their costs and make a profit, and those fee projections at the start of the project are quite important. But they rarely go as planned. When trying to plan out the costs of projects, the known outlays like wages and travel expenses are calculated, and a profit margin is added to try to ensure the company does not lose money.

Billing rates

Each employee in a company usually has a 'billing rate.' It is the fee that the company charges for that person's time. It is often calculated in direct proportion to their wages, which is then totalled up to show their projected hours on the project. That forms an approximate sum that it will cost for all the chosen staff to complete the job. Billing rates are often readily visible in company folders, set out on excel spreadsheets, divided into project roles, so you can easily discuss this with your management to understand it within a real setting. For example, a company director would have a very high hourly billing rate, followed by a project director, or project architect. It all helps to form a chart to calculate your overall project spend on staffing.

This is a whole separate world of business organisation, which can be fascinating from an operations side, but also quite dry. If you are not already sick of timesheets, you probably will be soon, but these are vital for companies planning their resourcing of staff onto other projects, depending on how much work is required on the current projects. When the company directors have 'resourcing meetings,' they are basically planning out which member of staff is going to be working on which project for this month and next, in order to plan out where projects need your skills. For example, your boss has most likely resourced you for the next couple of months.

Teams within your company

As your career progresses, perhaps to project architect or director level, you will spend far more of your time organizing and administering projects, instead of drawing and modelling them. In case you don't know it already, architects don't just wander into the office every day, take out a pencil and design buildings. There is so much more to do, unfortunately.

Project teams vary in size, but for large projects you might have teams working on manageable chunks of the building, split into packages, whilst the project architect organises meetings, data exchange with consultants, and submits reports to the client. There may be separate areas of the architect's business, like interior designers, and further down the line, specialist companies like façade engineers advising on glass types or detail junctions. Each company will be different here, but you will soon realise who does what in your company, and how projects are spread around quite a few people during different design stages.

A quick look at contracts

The contract you will most likely be exposed to is between the architect and client, or architect and main contractor. Get a copy of it. It is likely to be a long and seemingly complicated document, but it is worth requesting a few minutes with your project director to chat about it and learn the basics. When you take a good amount of time to read it properly, you should find that it is talking a lot of sense (hopefully), making responsibilities and deliverables very clear, and giving perfectly accurate clauses to be followed. Deliverables are the tasks, drawings, documents, reports or items that must be submitted, as outlined in the legal contract, in order for each company to declare that they have done their work and can be paid for it. Often, the next stage will not be able to start until those deliverables are met, but at the same time, there is often outstanding work that the project cannot wait for.

The contract is the document to refer back to when disputes start to build up, or clarifications are needed on exactly what you need to produce to complete your job, and therefore, get paid. I remember a contract I read, where materials and resources were forbidden to be sourced from a certain country, because of political tensions between them. There could be all sorts of strange rules and clauses in a contract. Try to find sections about deliverables, key project dates, project stages, payment schedule, late penalties, defects period, and dispute resolution. There is a lot to learn, which is not utterly crucial at the early stages in your career, but definitely take the opportunity to be inquisitive, make notes, and ask questions. Stay connected with how your project team is executing their deliverables. The more you can piece this all together, the better your overall understanding will be, and in my experience, the more motivation you feel from knowing exactly what the whole team is working towards.

Project stages

A project involves multiple company agreements and contracts, with overlapping terms, methods, strategies, and schedules, often all with their own acronyms, stages, and deliverables. Far too much to even summarise here. But you should appreciate that each company has their own little (or large) contribution to make, so if the team works better together, the project will be delivered more efficiently. A great place to start on project stages is the 'RIBA Plan of Work.'

Depending on what country you are in, there would hopefully be a similar diagram from the national architecture governing body. But anywhere in the world, the RPoW is a superb summary diagram, showing generally how construction projects go through different stages and what is required at each of them. It is a visual diagram, easy to search, and easy to understand broadly what is happening for an architect company to do the job, for which the client pays them.

Whilst keeping this summary very, very high level, the general project stages are: *project feasibility* to assess the viability, *project brief* to set out the requirements, *concept design*, *schematic design* to come up with the design solution, leading to the *developed design* and *final design*. The *construction phase* is followed by commissioning, then the big step of practical completion, and finally, the *handover* leading to full *occupation* of the final building. It is slightly different on all projects, so find out the phases to be completed according to your project contract. More recently, the measuring, data gathering, assessment, and feedback of the building performance is becoming more crucial to clients wanting to maximise their asset management. This is all about how the building owner can extract all the hard work and data that has gone into the project, and make their building operation phase more effective.

Key points:

•   Billing rates contribute to project planning, generally in line with your wages.

•   Contracts set out the deliverables, which are the tasks to be completed at each stage.

•   Projects are split into manageable chunks, for

easier execution, organisation and payment.

1.1.4 Attending meetings, project communication.

Any project meetings will be a great learning experience and something to look forward to. At the early stages, you probably won't have a great deal to communicate yourself, but learning from what other people say, how they say it, and who is fighting which corner is brilliant to see in action. You will possibly see a few heated debates too, which is always insightful because you really see each company protecting their own agenda. People care about their work, but they also care about their reputation, their job security, and money, so it is a potentially spectacular melting pot when project success is at stake.

Various types of meeting

Usually, on a weekly basis, there are client meetings, design team meetings, internal design chats, then sub-consultant, and subcontractor or supplier meetings. They can vary in frequency depending on the status of the project, with more meetings during the design phase, and a bit less in construction. The many design chats and team meetings within your own architecture company should be quite stimulating and inclusive; this is where you should be asking lots of questions. Jump at the chance to be involved in any meetings, even just observing whilst everyone else around the table talks and discusses the project.

Client meetings are usually pretty formal occasions, where only your company director or project architect would be attending, plus the main project runner for each of the consultant teams, like the structural company, mechanical and electrical company, the cost consultant, project manager, and perhaps any planning / statutory representative. The meeting content is mostly about updating the Client on progress, reporting major milestones coming up, and potentially raising difficulties or problems coming up. Sometimes companies won't reveal bad news to the client, because the design team would want to sort things out themselves in the background without causing any alarm unless there are huge ramifications or risks to discuss. Ideally, these are just check-ins with the client to say everything is going well, requesting guidance if needed, or confirming preferences for crucial decisions or budgets.

Design team meetings should be more effective for you to attend in the early years, even if just listening in. Typically, the chairperson of the meeting (project manager company or the architect's company) will start a quick formal introduction, outline what the meeting is trying to achieve, and maybe a quick introduction around the table from each person attending, so that everyone in the room knows who's who. This might go very quickly and you will not be able to remember everyone's name, but when it is your turn, just say your name and which company you work for, following the same style as the people before you.

Making progress via team meetings

At the start of the meeting, the chairperson will typically go through previous meeting minutes and discuss which actions have been completed or not, with any problems coming up. Ideally, items that were raised last week, should have been dealt with in the time between meetings but may need extra discussion with all the relevant people in the room to sort them out. It is great to see who leads the meetings and organises the agenda, splitting the design team from the project manager and cost consultant.

The design team arrange all the drawings and reports, whilst the cost consultant reports the financial position and risks, and the project manager, employed by the client, keeps the programme pushing along to ensure the building is on track to finish on time. It is definitely worth a few minutes chatting with your project architect so you know which company does what, and where the communication lines are in reference to the earlier diagram.

Key points:

• Team meetings keep everyone informed, focused and on track to complete their contractual deliverables.

• Jump at the chance to be involved in meetings, or writing minutes, especially on-site.

• Communication is paramount to success, so everyone needs that cohesive attitude.

1.1.5 Drawings 'where', schedules 'what', specs 'how'.

Projects are designed and delivered through project documentation. Simply put, that refers to all the documents you need to submit, in order to communicate everything about the design. These are drawings, diagrams, sketches, details, charts, reports, lists, schedules, real models, software models, site photos, and maps; everything.

Broadly, that documentation can be split into 3 parts:

- Drawings show *where* it is (and what it looks like).
- Schedules show *what* it is (naming exact products, materials, or colours).
- Specifications describe *how* to build it.

Project documentation uses any combination of those drawings, schedules, and specifications to best demonstrate the design so that it can be built. Separately, you can think of contracts as the legal overview of all 3 pieces of documentation.

You will mostly experience schedules in the form of a Materials Schedule, a Finishes Schedules, a Furniture Schedules, a Room Schedules and then the most commonly, the Window or Door schedules. For example, to document every door on the project, it is easier to have a huge chart showing all the doors, each being numbered, then featuring size, room, material, hinges, frame type, additional features like kick plates or edge seals, then vision panels, door hardware, and other comments. It's best to look one up online, or find your project version, as they are quite a daunting looking spreadsheet.

Finishes schedules are often very useful at early stages to show all the most visible finishes around the project in sensitive areas of the building, like the lobby or reception finishes, or finishes in the bathrooms or changing rooms.

These can be the items that make the project look really cool and professional when finished, hence why sometimes clients want that schedule early on in the project, to show the branding, platter of colours, or visual style.

The current combination of documentation

As with any part of the industry, remember that the way in which this information is shown is just the current best practice and most efficient way to communicate the design. In ten years' time, door schedules may have been superseded by a different, interactive, and inventive way to display all this information. But at the moment, the door schedule does a pretty good job at communicating all that information in one place, and generally, everyone understands it.

Similarly, with drawings or specifications, the industry currently follows these conventions of 'documentation' because it is familiar, it does the job, and it remains an organised way to arrange and display the information. The same principle goes for the details and coordination you will probably be involved in. Whichever arrangement, view, or style of drawing that best communicates the design to the main contractor, is going to be the one that is adopted. For example, I can see that model videos or 'flythroughs' as they are sometimes known, could soon be used more commonly to give a better 3D visualisation for a complicated piece of work, so that contractors and installers can understand the design intent. Other methods may soon gradually develop, but it is good to appreciate that the current 'documentation' is not the fixed and permanent way to do things. It is just indicative of what design and construction professionals currently find the most understandable and clear method of presenting the design.

Wonderful world of specifications

Specifications are typically seen as the boring part of projects because there is nothing visual about them. You may have only heard the occasional reference to specifications, as certainly was the case for me after more than five years in practice. Usually, specifications are hundreds of pages of writing and instructions, which never necessarily get looked at in full detail. Specifications are effectively the instruction manual for how to build the project. But they are legally crucial for ensuring basic levels of design, adherence to standards, and more often than not, have to be relied on so that the contractor gets the information they need. They are extremely important in avoiding discrepancies, and clearly identify instructions for fixings, installation, materials, or accessories that cannot really be shown on drawings.

Concerning the above point about prevalent methods to communicate design, specifications are going through a positive change now, whereby the document used to be a static article, purely written in Microsoft Word, and would rarely get used to its fullest. But now the integration of items in 'the spec' being directly linked to models is changing the way that products and installation are communicated. Specifications can now be easier divided into relevant sections and seen where needed, instead of thrown together in one huge file.

Understanding the accuracy of documentation

My analogy for understanding specifications is like ordering a coffee. So, in this case, what is your personal specification for ordering a coffee at a cafe? Maybe you just look up at the pictures on the board, know roughly what you like, and choose that. The options are pretty simple. Would you like a large or small, black or white, with any sugar or not? That's your simple coffee order. That's your coffee specification.

But there is far more to a coffee order than that; a better specification would be to state whether you would like a small - 250ml, medium - 350ml, or large - 450ml coffee? Would you like coffee beans freshly ground or the pre-packed granules? White or brown sugar? Is there almond milk or soy milk to choose from? Would you like it stirred once all the ingredients are in, or only when the coffee mixes with milk? You can see here there has been a lot more detail that you would not necessarily have thought about with the first simple order, but you have got a far more exact version of the coffee you want, so the output is likely to be better due to this specification.

The next level of specification could really get detailed, for example, is it a takeaway coffee or sit in? Would you like it in a paper cup or ceramic? Because this changes how quickly it gets cold. Coffee beans from the middle east or south America? Would you like the milk warmed first? Would you like it frothed? Full cream milk, skimmed, almond milk, or soy? Would you like the coffee made separately first, before adding the milk, or throw it all in together from a packet and then the hot water? Sugar added at the end or left for you to do it yourself? Finally, would you like it with a lid or left open?

Hopefully, you can appreciate that the specification

gives exact requirements for every parameter you can think of. For another food analogy, your recipe might say apple pie, but there are at least six different varieties I can think of, so clarification of which type is key. High-quality apples? Yes, but high quality by whose standards? This is open to interpretation, so the specification could say, 'Six Golden Delicious apples, fully ripened to pure green, at a minimum total weight of 3kg.' I can brainstorm the following items that would all be open to dangerous interpretation if you were not exact about it. So, your specification would need to accurately state all the details.

• Dimensions: overall height, the height of just the pie not including the plate it sits on, dimensions of each layer of pastry, the thickness of the filling, a perfect circle or oval shape, and overall diameter of the pie.

• Apples: from a certain supermarket, originally from France, Pink Lady type, full green colour to ensure ripeness, a minimum diameter for each apple, no visible blemishes to the skin, and not to be past the sell-by date.

• Appearance: completely covered in powdered sugar, show no indication of knife or spatula marks, totally smooth pastry finish, evenly spread filling to all areas, ensure a flat top, not a dome shape, and do not spill powdered sugar onto the outside of the plate.

• Additional: provide a small 200ml tub of spare powdered sugar. Pie to be presented in a clean cardboard box in a cube shape so that the pie does not touch the inside of the box, apart from its base. Use tape to secure the box.

As you can see here just for a simple product, I can be extremely specific about what I want, and conversely, if not communicated, can cause misinterpretation, and therefore, an incorrect final product. If any of those things were not stated at the start, you cannot really complain when the end result is just a little bit different from the order. Take this approach to the thousands of products involved in a building project, and you can see why specifications are so crucial, and why they are often hundreds of pages long.

Efficiency of information

So, what you cannot show on a drawing can be covered in the specification and described further by a schedule. The key for all documentation is, of course, consistency. They should work in unison to show the right things, in the right place to avoid discrepancy. Most of the crucial installation information is often loaded into the specification and actually made far more efficient by doing this. You can establish rules for all instances within the entire project, just by capturing it once in the specification, instead of trying to annotate that on every drawing where that item is shown.

Generally, architects have no idea how many times they have been saved by having a decent standardized specification to back up their drawings. It is a good thing to spend some time looking through a spec once you are into a project. It will be a serious mental workout but go through it slowly and it will all make sense, especially if you were to have the related drawings with you. I currently work in the specifications world, so get in touch if you have some questions.

Influence of technology

Considering the increasingly digital world that projects are executed in, you would think that all this project documentation should be really well synchronised and organised to allow maximum efficiency and effectiveness of the data. BIM has definitely enabled and improved that, but the transition is still slow. Strangely, the construction industry has not really adopted technology and connectivity en-masse, in the way it should or could have done. Risk probably plays a factor, in terms of companies not wanting to try anything new or unproven. Working attitudes and adaptation can take too long to learn, and therefore, liability and delays become too risky to take.

Change management is a huge factor for any company in any industry, but perhaps architects being traditionally careful, logical, methodical, and risk-averse kind of people, are not great at jumping into new things. Hopefully, that is changing. But the power of building models should be exploited, better connected, and accessed by the rest of the project team, instead of still being independently shown and extracted on an excel spreadsheet or word files. I suppose this is the essence, which means more of the wider project team becoming familiar and comfortable with using BIM models. The industry is changing by adopting excellent software to help connectivity and integration. That's bound to be a big growth area too, and hence a progressive part of the industry for you to specialise in.

On well-equipped building sites, automation should be quite common. Contractors may have iPads or tablets ready in the site office, or in use 50 storeys up, to check through thousands of drawings on a linked document management website at any time. Due to our current networks of connectivity, site staff can instantly look up specifications and finishes for any location, via spec-to-model integrations that are becoming common. Accessing the BIM model from that on-site device should allow you to navigate, find and search any tiny little detail about the project, and supply instant photos, reports, and remedies to site issues. It should massively speed up the construction process, and main contractor companies are likely to be researching these benefits very closely in order to cut costs on their operations.

In my career so far, I have seen a massive improvement in the technical capabilities of main contractors, and their increasingly savvy understanding of the software allows them to control more of the project, and benefit financially from building efficiencies. The vast majority of the money on projects goes into the construction phase, so improvements there are of utmost important. It is not necessary to reinvent the wheel on these technological advances, but the possibilities seem really endless at the moment, as discussed in section 2 about the future of architecture.

Updating information

In any project, it is inevitable that information from drawings, schedules, and specifications, will not all match up 100% of the time. When the design changes or substitutions (like variations) are suggested by your main contractor, the updating of information is a job in itself, even despite it being in theory quite easy to track and remedy with the connectivity as discussed. Main contractors are more and more crucial in driving this, along with clients and facilities managers. I will not go into too much detail here, but there is a recent trend of contractors improving their in-house BIM knowledge by employing qualified architects and technologists to better extract the information in the model, and apply design changes themselves as effectively as the design team would usually do. It's pretty obvious to realise that if a company has more building expertise, then they can solve more of the problems themselves and complete more of the design themselves. As discussed earlier, this threatens the role of the traditional architect even further.

How do we control innovation and technology?

So, is the technological influence all positive? The bigger the project, the more information there is, the more specific and unique details there are, and therefore, the more people that are involved. From that point of view, there are more tasks that require detailed attention, therefore, more things that can go wrong. Technology undoubtedly helps us remedy that, and very rarely will a computer system make a computing error. From one viewpoint, you can say humans are the problem. Keeping all drawings consistent and fully up to date, daily, with constantly amended project information, and every other drawing that relates to that item becomes difficult to track. You can employ more people and have staff to purely manage the updating process, but mistakes will inevitably occur. Surely that has been made far easier by BIM data. More avenues of information require more input, organisation and control, which needs more employees, which allows and creates more problems.

It's interesting to consider what level of technological application becomes too much and infringes humans from doing their job. Technology needs to improve the output of a human, or do it quicker, or both. But do humans need to first improve the output of the computer? You might find that project organisation relies so heavily on technology, that you feel quite distant from the actual building on some days.

Can you make the change?

The variety of documentation items should all be up to date with each other. That challenge still exists, but the way in which it is done will change. Technology will improve, innovations will be made, but until companies embrace those different options and succeed with them, then the typical combination of drawings, schedules, and specifications remains the best way to complete the deliverables of the contract. If you can personally invent or develop any better or more integrated ways of communicating the design to the contractor and wider team, you will be a saviour of the construction industry!

Key points:

• Projects are executed from a combination of drawings, schedules, and specifications.

• Until there is a better way to communicate the design, this is the current status.

• Advancement of technology should always benefit

projects, not be overcomplicated.

• If there are better, cheaper, more efficient options available, companies will soon adopt them.

1.1.6 Seeing the design process evolve

I have really enjoyed seeing projects develop from early-stage design, move into construction phase, and continue all the way until completion and handover. It is quite unusual to be directly involved right from the start until right to the finish, but if there is ever the opportunity to do that, and see the work right through until occupation and feedback, put your hand up to be involved. The project will likely be the result of hundreds, maybe thousands, of people's effort and dedication over months or years. So to witness all that and learn from the good, bad, stressful, and worrying, but hopefully uplifting, and overall proud moment to see it finished, is hugely exciting. There should be as much enjoyment in the journey as well as the destination.

In my years of professional work, and therefore about 35-40 projects, I think I have only seen a project to the finish four or five times. The ratios are probably far better in smaller architect practices, with shorter, smaller projects. But in the larger firms, I've worked at, the massive projects are far more likely to run into a wide range of problems with financing, political, or economic effects, pauses in the process or purely the length of time they are active projects. You might not be at that company long enough to see it through. But seeing this design process in action is fantastic, and as mentioned earlier, architecture is simply about designing and constructing buildings, so it's the real essence of what you do. You will encounter lots of talented designers in your career, and plenty of amazing building designs, options, and concept ideas that do not progress into a real project. They are all part of the journey of design. Witnessing that evolution of ideas should demonstrate a very good lesson, and a phrase I often still use now, there is no such thing as a perfect project.

The design process is a journey

The design process, in its most basic form, is not difficult to understand. I really enjoy this part of the industry because you are involved in the process of identifying a need or problem and satisfying it with a response. It uses spatial and data analysis, design ideas and improvement, and evolution of thinking relating to client preferences. You and your team will be changing and amending models and drawings to reflect this process, to gradually get closer to the right design, and therefore, the right response. Whilst outside factors change and variables of the project come and go, the final design becomes the optimal result of all the influences mixed together and gradually shaped into the best solution. It's very difficult to design or draw something perfectly the first time. A refinement process helps to keep improving on your first thoughts, with other specialists helping you to determine improvements and efficiencies. However, the process of design can mean many different things and have many different results.

The design output (in this case a building) is an interpretation of how to arrange and create something from set instructions and boundaries. Therefore, each designer might have a slightly different process, method, or result, because you are dealing with the output of opinions, personalities, and cultural upbringing. Give 10 designers a simple brief to design a house, and you can be sure there will be 10 very different interpretations of how best to satisfy that brief. As you will see in this book there are many influences on projects, all trying to achieve slightly different things, all dipping their fingers into the various facets of the design. So, perhaps designing a building is more of a human process, a reflection on personality, an extension of your brain, and an interpretation of the world. A building is the result of all that.

In its most basic intention, the design process is trying to achieve an optimum solution to a problem. The design process should push efficiency and quality to its limit whilst satisfying the client requirements. The design will change, evolve, and attempt to be the best it can be at various stages. Each small client decision will usually be followed by changes in the design, so expect much to change from week to week. It is a winding pathway, anything but a straight road. The design process can be swift and clear when the time frame or variables are small, or the design process can take place over months and years when the architectural result is being interrogated, investigated, and moulded by many people and factors.

The design process in project form

Contractually, it is important to know that you should not go beyond those deliverables as discussed, and of course, financially there is a crucial reason to just do the work, drawings, or studies as required by the stage. You will see this at its most effective through concept design or design development, often called 'schematic design,' where you will need to produce a pre-set list of drawings to communicate the design in enough detail to move towards the next stage. The project runner and company directors will be (should be) on top of exactly when you complete your stage of work, and what level of drawings need to be finalised. So, even when there are boundaries, even if there is a rigid framework to operate in, the design process is still happening to find the best result. The project stage effectively determines what level of detail you need to show of the building.

Efficiency of design can be particularly important in commercial and retail projects. Using every little square foot of floor space is the challenge. Making every ceiling height as generous as possible for optimized light and space. Tiny improvements on floor areas can improve the rentable income potential for your client in a commercial office situation. This reflects very well on your design team if you can keep finding small areas of the building to expand floor area. That means more pounds or dollars per square foot for leasing purposes, totalling potentially millions more in revenue over the long life of a client's asset.

The design process is not infallible

If ever you are taking a look around the site near completion, it is interesting to realise how it compares to the original design. There has most likely been a lot of compromises, plenty of change, and a fair bit of total redesign compared to the original. In my London renovation projects, covering up ugly pipework with plasterboard, or hiding old structural oddities behind feature walls, or just plainly trying detail around an error, was very common. Miscalculations or misjudgments where you were already tight for space is always an interesting puzzle to solve and sometimes results in a creative solution for construction detailing. This is where the real fun and ingenuity of design comes through because it is not always the pure design process that works so well on paper.

If you can ever get some site work, absolutely grab it with two hands. It is a highly educational experience; you will be exposed to the quite blunt style of builders and main contractors. To be quite stereotypical, they often don't care much about the architecture of the project. Their prime concern is to build the project in line with the design, then potentially replace items for cheaper equivalents as discussed with value engineering, if it suits their balance sheet. Being in the architectural profession means you really care about every last detail of your project, but understand that not everyone will be of that mindset. It is crucial for your development to see how many hands are dipping into your project, and how your knowledge and negotiating skills will affect the outcome right until the very last moments.

Hopefully, you can see this design process as an overall and necessary part of the project. Over a few years, you will probably form your own version and interpretation of the design process. Many companies hold this phrase in very high regard, like some sort of company ethic or deep help mission statement. You will be able to find a few very thick books to debate and hypothesise about the whole thing if you have the time to read about the theory and importance of design.

In my interpretation, the design process starts as soon as you engage with the project client to establish what sort of building, they want. Instantly, you are finding out what sort of person they are, or what sort of building they want, which all affects your design solution. That design process will twist and turn continually, until the final installation of the project, and the building is finally opened. It might still be ongoing once changes and adaptations are required during occupation. Once you start using the building, it becomes clear that little amendments could help, so the design process is always adapting to that too.

You will come across many other phrases preaching the enlightenment or understanding of the secret to good design. This can be quite aspirational in my experience, but remember the bottom line is that architecture is a deliberate process, addressing a need and trying to satisfy it with a solution. Whatever you are involved in will be slightly different each time, but that's all part of the excitement of your next 'perfect' project.

Key points:

•   It will be hugely educational if you can remain on a project all the way through.

•   What is design; a moment or a process?

•   Companies use their design ethos principles as a very powerful message to their clients.

1.1.7 A summary of project roles

If this book were written 30 years ago, the following list would be barely half as long. The nature of the industry has diluted so many roles, therefore it is useful to know who the major players are and what they do. I have listed them out below with short descriptions. The first list is considered more as the absolute essentials because almost every project will have them. There will of course be anomalies to that, and it is just from my experience. The second list is still hugely important in executing projects, but a little less common, therefore, not crucial to deeply understand at the early stages of your career.

The obvious roles in a project are the client or developer, being either the owner of the land or the company being employed by the client to execute the overall project. Then, of course, the 'design team,' which broadly consists of the architect, structural engineer, mechanical engineer (often this 'Building Services' company includes mechanical, electrical, and plumbing, hence M.E.P.), sustainability consultant, and fire engineer. Then the project manager, cost consultant, and planning department are often engaged by the client. As always, check out your own project contract or responsibility matrix diagram within your company folders, which should list or show the companies involved in your current project.

Architect – historically, the architect (defined as Chief Builder) was the project leader, had all the answers, made all the decisions, and was a hugely admired job. Whilst still a crucial and well-respected job in society, it has been diluted in the past few decades, in my experience. Currently, lots of jobs are arranged with the architect company as the 'Lead Designer,' hence, still holding a position of authority in the design team, and ultimately responsible for how the building looks and how it is used.

Project Director / Project Leader – this person may be managing many projects at once within your company. They do most of the client communication, organize the architectural team, make most of the big decisions, and of course, manage all the financial agreements, effectively having a hand in all the high-level aspects of the project. Usually with many years of professional experience, they should know the industry extremely well and have lots of company duties, aside from just the project execution.

Project Architect / Runner – this is the authentic architect's job, the day-to-day hands-on architect. Typically aged about 28 years old and onwards, having completed the full architectural qualification with some professional experience for 4 / 5 years. Project architects primarily organise the drawing submissions, manage the team in-house, and organise the design team consultants below them, and report back to the client.

Fire Engineer – a specialist (or department within the Services company) employed to analyse, document and solve complex fire risks, restrictions, escape routes, ratings of walls, the function of sprinklers, and Fire Brigade access. This can potentially use hugely complicated diagrams, simulators, exit paths, times, and strategies for phases of evacuation. Lots of this knowledge would be expected from a qualified architect, but bigger complex projects require someone who knows all the finer details about how sprinkler systems affect the nature of the fire strategy, and how computer modelling can help show how people would escape in phases within the building in an event of a fire. An absolutely crucial part of any design because of the risk and damage caused by fires.

Structural Engineer – obviously employed to make sure the building is going to stand up. A bit like the bones in your body. Structural engineers allow a lot of the magic of design to happen by calculating how stresses and forces of buildings allow amazing cantilevers, huge spans, and create large spaces. All the science behind concrete, steel, and timber physics is responsible for constructing a rigid and safe building, whilst it is being constructed, as well as during the life-time of the building.

MEP Engineer (Mechanical, Electrical, Plumbing) – employed to design, coordinate and synchronise the services in or around the building. If the structure of the human body is the bones, then think of MEP in the body as all the veins, vessels, muscles, and nerves taking blood around your body and connecting to your heart, lungs, stomach, etc. Coordination of this role is crucial for allowing enough room for all the pipework, cabling, and ductwork. In turn, that affects things like the precious ceiling heights for apartments, location of electricity points, the amount of shaft space needed in core layouts, or the power connections to serve the whole building.

Landscape Architect – a stylish landscape design can make an amazing difference to the visual impact of the project, but more so now with energy and sustainability credentials so closely aligned with this role. This design is not just greenery, but also paving, drainage, water capture and reuse, pathways, shared podium areas like residential shared pools or communal gardens, everything on the site which is not the building footprint. This usually includes balconies and roof gardens, but that scope may be solely the architect's responsibility. The late 1990s and 2000s saw a huge drive in the UK for vegetation on roofs of buildings.

Building Surveyor / Building Control – ensuring the building adheres to building regulations, the building surveyor will assess the design for the overall use of the occupants, and question badly designed areas. This usually requires sign off at various stages.

Quantity Surveyor – tabulating all the material quantities in the building, and therefore, making various calculations that feed into cost estimates and orders. Think of the massive shopping list created by a building design, this all needs to be tabulated and controlled so that spending does not get out of hand, and can sometimes be 'value engineered' as the project progresses. Often done at a very high level in early stages to give approximate predictions, sums of money can be reserved for certain things which are not known yet, which is a 'provisional sum.'

Builder / Main Contractor – the company who is building the project, thus, has a massive impact on the result of architecture. The Main Contractor will employ lots of subcontractors directly to accomplish specialist parts of the work. The relationship between client, architect, and the main contractor is the most important of all. The main contractor wants to safely execute the build, and do it with profit. Thus, they will try to make substitutions for products or designs if it makes their life easier to build it or is cheaper. This company should be bringing building expertise and an excellent understanding of construction efficiency to the project.

Subcontractor – diagrammatically one step below the main contractor, this company is more focused on one single item, e.g.: tiled floors, carpet floors, window installations, ceilings, doors, or sanitary fittings. They have been given the overall design intent by the architect, but will often produce 'shop drawings,' which interpret the design ready for construction so that the architect can sign off what is being proposed.

Cost Consultant – this company looks after the money, cost projections, and budget. Sometimes combined within the project management company, and typically very close to the client, to be constantly reporting back how much the project is going to cost, at various stages. So they rely heavily on the architect's drawings and product selections to make these estimations. As mentioned earlier, the entire industry does still come down to money, so the cost estimation of projects and ongoing control of them is massive.

Project Manager – effectively an organiser of tasks to be done. This is a role that came into effect mostly in the late 80s in terms of UK construction, but it is very popular now. They are employed to ensure the smooth running of the project, and to keep it on time, communicating deadlines, and requirements from all the people and companies involved. Daily production of spreadsheets, programmes, charts, and dates to keep everything on track.

It is difficult to be sure of exactly who would be on your project, but broadly those are the companies and people you should know about. Further project disciplines are listed below, which are a little less common. Hopefully, they would not all be present on one project, but it is good to appreciate their specialism and why the project would need their services.

Accessibility Advisor – there may be varied terminology of this role around the world, but the reason for this consultant is to ensure everyone in society can freely move around a building. This consultant advises on things like handrail heights, gradients of ramps, turning circles, corridor widths, setting out of all bathroom accessories, ease of access, and safe zones for the fire escapes (To Part M in the UK, or adhering to AS 1428.1 in Australia). As a good architectural professional, you should know most of this anyway, but on larger complex buildings an Accessibility Advisor can be employed at an early stage for general compliance, then later on for detailed checks to ensure sign off.

Architectural Assistant / Graduate Architect – this will most likely be the title of your first job out of university, or something similar. This role is like an extension of the architect where you will assist them, usually producing drawings, studies, or reports to feed into main submissions and project communication. A huge amount of work will be 'coordination' which is all the fine tuning and optimising the building design, with your other consultants in the design team.

Document Controller – depending on the number of drawings, reports, documents, and spreadsheets being sent around the team, this role might be for just one project, or the whole company. It is hugely important for smooth running and rigid organisation of projects, by organising various online uploads and transfers of documents to the right person or company so that each person has the right information to do their job.

Site Architect – the only difference to a regular architect role being that they are stationed almost solely on-site, responsible for executing the design that would have already been agreed upon beforehand. So, this role is focused on needing to protect the design intent of the architect, whilst the main contractor might be trying to change things due to cost savings or site constraints.

Civil Engineer – infrastructure specialist for design and coordination of roads, railways, sewerage, cabling, and drainage. This is obviously crucial to connect power and sewerage to the building and coordinate all the on-site works below ground.

Environmental / Sustainability Consultant – responsible for ensuring the project has sustainable credentials and positively contributes to environmental targets. This is a huge subject, so there are globally recognized certificates and achievements that are very common now, based on rating systems like BREEAM, LEED, or Green Star. If your building performs well in terms of energy usage and is a healthy building for occupants to live or work in, then the owner of the building can charge more rent for those who use it. Thus, this environmentally sensitive role does still partly come down to money.

Geotech Consultant – specialist consultant for understanding and recommending the strategy for ground conditions, and therefore, foundations, e.g.: rock, sand, clay, and risk of watery or sludgy ground. Works closely with structural engineers for the building foundations and substructure. Search terms like piling, water table, liquefaction, and bedrock for a bit more information.

Heritage Consultants – many buildings require protection from development, or sensitive design and refurbishment when it needs to happen, because of their historical value. Often due to the government or local council laws, how to deal with and care for old buildings with heritage value is hugely important. Amazingly historical cities like London, Rome, or Athens (and, of course, many others around the world) are so popular because that history has been retained, preserved, and showcased.

Hydraulic Engineer – involved with water movement and pumping, whether that be for toilets, showers, rainwater storage, or pumps. Often a specialist subject within the plumbing part of the MEP engineer.

Interior Designer – a massive industry by itself and huge cross over with the architect, coordinating the interior finishes in the building. Very important in hotels and offices, to get that wow factor in lobbies for example, but also domestic or residential buildings, choosing materials and tones that complement each other and create ambience.

Ecologist – works closely with the Environmental engineer to assess the value and impact of the land, in terms of animals, insects, plant species, ecosystems, and the impact of development against displacement. Ecology reports have been known to legally stop huge projects because of a species of animal that would need to be rehoused before digging up the earth and destroying their habitat.

Specification Writer – projects are effectively made of three parts of documentation; drawings show you *where*, schedules show you *what*, and specifications show you *how*. Specifications are usually hundreds of pages long like an instruction manual for how to build a building. They are complex and need to be extremely accurate, covering products, materials, standards, regulations, execution, and installation, then care and maintenance of the asset going forward.

Concept Architect - some architectural firms survive almost solely on conceptual design work, visually amazing designs that clients like to publicise as their next building, but in reality, won't always end up completely loyal to that early concept. Most famous architects have broken new ground with very original and stunning looking buildings.

Technical Architect – focused a little more on the technical, scientific, and buildability side of architecture. Not always a qualified architect, but they should know the current industry very well, how products are made and put together, and also be up to date regarding the latest building regulations and legislation.

Graphic Designers – purely focused on the graphical and presentation side, often on the marketing side of the business, good at making the 3D shots of the building look even better for company brochures, and press release images,

Town Planner – understanding the context of your project and the impact of how the building sits within the street, district, town, or whole country. Town planning organisations look at the overall impact on all the local people, business, green space, social fabric, and how these things should be organised. The success of towns and cities is generally down to good planning.

Waste Collection Consultant – often under the MEP engineer scope. All the usual garbage and waste has to be moved around and eventually picked up by the refuse collection service, so it is especially crucial in residential tower projects, hotels or large offices. Design considerations will be how and exactly where to collect it, truck access and turning space, or compaction machines and drainage.

Design Manager - usually, on the contractor side but now more commonly in the architect's company as well, this person really focuses on design. Likely to be very talented at designing spaces, increasing efficiency of design, knowing good buildability, and being able to push the boundaries of the very best design outcomes.

Traffic Consultant – on any size schemes, incoming and outgoing vehicles is crucial, for residents, users, waste collection cyclists, emergency services, etc. Especially important in high rise projects and tight inner-city projects where the project ratios needed are quite testing. This often links into the overall city or town planning department to ensure road capacity is sufficient, and the design adheres to the road width regulations.

Aviation Consultant – if your project is near an airport, it will be crucial to install lighting beacons on top of tall buildings to adhere to height restrictions. If you get this wrong, the building design may not be permitted by the local authority.

Key points:

• Concentrate on the companies involved in your current project, to see the basics.

• Find out what each company does, and who is directly employing them.

• Ensure project understanding by chatting to your colleagues.

1.2 BUILDING YOUR CAREER IN ARCHITECTURE

1.2.1 CV, portfolio, website, profiles, interviews.

1.2.2 A job and career to be enjoyed not endured.

1.2.3 Experiencing negatives, problems, and change.

1.2.4 Office folk - the good, bad, and the ugly.

1.2.5 Choosing a company to work for.

1.2.1 CV, portfolio, website, profiles, interviews.

The need to produce an amazing CV when applying for jobs has never really gone away and is the same in the architectural world. However, in recent years within the architecture profession, a CV is now just part of a spread of items needed to represent yourself, alongside a portfolio, website, and additional online profiles. There is so much (maybe too much) advice on the internet, and therefore, so much pressure on ensuring a really impressive CV and portfolio, but I think getting the basics right is not that hard. The unrelenting and never-ending advice available online is very daunting, so I think there is a balance to be achieved on not getting addicted to it, and tick the main boxes first. Take advice from diverse sources, don't compare yourself too much with the '10 best ever architectural CVs,' and remember the fundamental aspects you are conveying. You just want to demonstrate what you can do for a company, with a hint of your personality and style to the documents you are sending. Commonly now, the on-screen representation of your skills has become so visually driven by stunning project examples, that unfortunately, the lengths you can go to for CV design are never-ending. Hopefully, I can make it a little easier for you, as below.

The basics of a CV and portfolio

A fairly rigid 2-page CV layout can definitely cover what you need to communicate. In my early years, 2 pages were the absolute maximum, and sometimes just 1 page was enough, with a few smart drawings to take along to an interview, having attached them to my application email.

But now, the standard has risen unbelievably high. The imagery and printing quality is pretty amazing, and the quality of student portfolio work is superb. The presentation standards are getting pushed higher and higher, so as a minimum, you need a punchy CV and really impressive portfolio. Getting some good quality prints will be well worth the small financial outlay.

Your first challenge is to decide how far to push these items. As noted above, a CV and portfolio is the minimum, with a personal website, and online profiles being a great addition if you can manage these too. If you go for a personal website too, remember it can be mostly an extension, and combination, of the CV and portfolio, but will need to be very visually engaging to browse through on various devices. Large blocks of writing will generally not be read, so clear and very succinct notes can be enough. The pictures and drawings should simply represent the sort of work you can produce, which is the main thing you are communicating. Concerning online profiles, I personally think a LinkedIn profile is great to wrap this all together in a recognisable and clearly set out format. However, the content is obviously simpler and less visual, so if in doubt, keep it simple and don't risk contradictions or discrepancies with your CV information.

Concerning CV content, you can certainly take some inspiration from all the online examples you can find, because they look so stylish and present information in attractive, original ways. But from my experience, clarity of information is at the top of the priorities list. The CV should, of course, convey your personal style in an attention-grabbing design, but displaying your best information in the clearest way is paramount. These subtle design choices on the CV page are strangely influential in creating the vibe of your CV.

Just think of the style and colour of restaurant signage, food packaging or product advertising. It all creates an atmosphere to convey the quality, professionalism, or price of the product you have. So the font choice, text size, information arrangement, and clarity of that information all paint a picture about how you describe yourself on a blank page of paper.

To look at it from the other side of the table, your CV will be disregarded very quickly if it is badly organised, not logically aligned on the page, and not consistently arranged. If your skills or education details are hard to find, are poorly presented, or have simple errors, you cannot blame someone for thinking your professional work will be similar. Simple spelling mistakes are really disastrous. They are so easy to remedy with spell check, yet, so many applications make basic errors. That conveys to a prospective company that you are not going to check important bits of work, and you are not going to clean up your own errors. Clearly you are not going to get that job.

For layout tips, I think your basic personal details, like name, DOB, contact email, or number, and, possibly, nationality, should be at the top of the page. Keep it brief, followed by a short profile of yourself in only three or four bullet points. These should be the absolute headline things about you and your capabilities. But the most important bits come next. I would say your professional experience is most important, followed by your educational qualifications. That's the real top-level information that companies want to see, to decide if you are even employable. If your education is the best, but you cannot talk of much experience, it is difficult for a company to know what to do with you. However, if your education was years ago, but your experience is fantastic and relevant, I think the day-to-day skills will prove more influential, so it is best to push that to prime position on the CV.

A common issue that I have mentees raise with me, was the fact it was so hard to get experience on your CV if no companies will employ you to start with. It is a really hard situation to be in, but if you can get any sort of work experience before university, or in summer placements, you really must take it. You will probably be on low wages, but that cannot be a priority at this early stage, just get any small amount of work in practice, and soon it will build up. Failing that, any sort of self-learning or online software courses you can take in the downtime would be a good representation of your attitude.

Back to the CV, and the next section is about your additional office responsibilities or involvement, followed by software skills, and then personal interests and references. A professional black and white headshot photo near the top corner is quite common now and you will see quite a lot of colour added to CVs compared to the black and white only from previous years.

Over recent years I have seen 3-page CVs, featuring a very detailed list of experience, documenting all projects, and many dissected responsibilities. From the company's point of view, there can be a huge mixture of applicants for a role, with a very wide range of qualifications, from all manner of educational institutes. It can therefore be very difficult to compare education standards and knowledge levels, hence the universities need to be rigorously assessed against each other.

So, gauging your own local market is important to know where you sit. If you want to further communicate your project experience, I think it would be appropriate to attach a heavily detailed projects profile to your application, but only as an appendix to the CV, if you have enough experience to warrant that. But be aware this may be an overload for the reader, because you still should be able to document your professional experience quickly and succinctly like everyone else does. As a general rule about the current industry, anything goes now in terms of selling yourself, as long as it is manageable, clear, and shows what applicable skills you can bring to a company.

Get the basics right, quality over quantity

To summarise, I would say three things are definitely top of the list: 1. show them your best skills, capabilities, i.e., what role you can actually perform for this company; 2 – give a clear representation of your current experience in the field, and 3 – declare your official education and qualifications logically listed. Once the reader has absorbed that information, the portfolio style and quality need to take over and knock their socks off with clear, relevant imagery and examples of your output. They must be your drawings, or at least drawings that you directly contributed to which you can explain. Quality, not quantity here, and ensure you can explain the good and bad about the designs or details you are talking about. The company will want to hear about your experience, and they will already know that projects can be positive as well as negative, so over both bases there.

As for portfolios, they should, of course, be colour printed (unless you are going for a stylish black and white theme) in high quality if you can, with interesting elevations, sections, 3Ds, details, sketches, and theoretical information. Each piece of information on your portfolio should be contributing to the overall impact. Do not add anything that is a bit average, or that you are not proud of. Everything should show your skills at their best. Use logical fonts (probably to match your CV font), well-sized, sensibly arranged, making any blocks of writing line up and balance nicely on the page. Don't overhype or over-annotate the portfolio. It is a visual study, just a few important notes or annotations are okay. Don't just describe what can already be seen. Communicate the process of the design you went through, what were the inspirations and influences that made it end up this way.

Also consider who is reading your information. Firstly, human resources or administration employees will be the first checkpoint to get through. They will probably disregard CVs that are untidy, include easy mistakes or don't communicate your main points quickly. Then the important viewers will likely be the project architects or decision-makers. Remember from their point of view, it is a big decision too. They are considering whether to pay you thousands of pounds or dollars over a number of months ahead, and gauging the impact you will have on their team or the company.

The next step up in the process will be the company directors, who will not have a lot of time to check you out. They might do it whilst commuting home, via a mobile phone, or small laptop, and they might forward snapshots to other members of their team for their opinion. So, you might need to test that your information loads correctly via attachments or PDFs, or when displayed on various screen sizes, or if you are sending a website link. Large companies typically look through a couple of hundred CVs each week, and unfortunately the smallest things may put them off. So, the absolute priority is to make sure it is visually engaging, easily understood, and shows what you can do.

Put yourself on the other side of the table

Discrepancies between your information would be a really easy and negative mistake to make. It is often easy to spot mistakes in colleagues' work with a fresh pair of eyes, but it makes you think they did not bother to evaluate their own work. Analyse the overall package of yourself that you are presenting. Would you prefer a small amount of information that is perfectly organised and consistent? Or lots of information but is misleading, confusing, and contradictory. The bottom line is that the employer just wants to know within a few minutes what you are like, and whether you can do the job they need. Think about what the person on the other side of the table is looking for. If you were hiring architectural staff, what would you look for?

One final thing to say, is to be patient after you have sent applications. The fact is that plenty of companies will not quite engage with your CV in the same way as others will, and some companies might not need your skills at the moment. You should wait for a week until bugging the company again about your application. A week can go very quickly in the industry and the decision makers will likely be short of time. You definitely need to be a little bit prepared for a feeling of rejection here, because if you were a company director and had one position to fill but ten applicants, the fact is that you will have to disappoint nine people, regardless of how brilliant their CVs and portfolios were. So, your own positivity and optimism is crucial to remaining persistent and dedicated, knowing that somewhere along the line you will find a good company to work for.

How to crack the interview

Attending an interview is definitely going to be a scary prospect if you are a bit nervous. Unfortunately, the best advice is to not be nervous. It is a very normal feeling of course, because an interview is a big deal, and you want it to go well, but anxiety or worry will stop you from giving a good performance. You will just have to 'switch off' your nervousness for a short time if you can. Does your employer want a nervous, frightened employee? Do they want someone who is going to crumble or freeze when the pressure is on? You cannot project yourself very well if you are too nervous to chat. It will be difficult to snap yourself out of nerves or anxiety, but keep imagining yourself on the other side of the table. How would you like this interview to go? If you are getting to know someone who might potentially work for your company, you would want to see them as a well-balanced, intelligent, and nice person first of all. Be bright, engaging, and interesting but professional, so that the company can really get to know you from that personal level. If you have made it to an interview, then they already like your qualifications and experience, so just be natural, friendly, and sensible.

I gave some good advice during mentoring a few years back regarding interviews. Basically, treat an interview as an informal chat. You are just talking to another human being about a subject you both like, so it is not too difficult. If the vibe you give out is worried, unstable, or scared, it will transmit to what you would be like in their office. It can be an intense process if you are a bit shy and talking to an expert, but you have to remain calm and project yourself as someone who can help their company. If your personality is more outgoing and extroverted, you can discuss all the extra skills and aspects of office life you would be involved in and contribute to. Either way, just like meeting anyone new in life, they need to get a fair and honest view of what you would be like as their team mate.

Body language is key, so practice being relaxed and open in conversation, but also responsible and serious. No slouching and no darting your eyes around the room. This is a relatively ordinary situation that they have to do many times a year. If you end up working for this company, you will be involved in hundreds of quick team chats over the next few months and years, so don't get off to a bad start by not being able to sit there and hold a conversation. They just want to get to know you. So, allow that to happen, speak kindly and honestly, and if you don't know how to answer a question, be proactive and say you are not sure, but you would be inquisitive and motivated to find the answer from colleagues.

You will likely be asked to expand on the details of your CV, and chat through your experiences, so prepare a couple of bullet points for each project, on small note cards if you want, to show you are organised and prepared. I have had mostly good interviews, where I managed to calmly talk about my CV and portfolio, but one particularly bad experience was a second interview. I think I had pretty much secured the job already, but had to revisit the studio to meet the Managing Director in person. I guess I was a little more nervous than in the previous interview, but after only about five minutes, he asked me why I looked so anxious and unsure of myself. The problem was, that I thought I was doing fine, but the fact he thought I was nervous, made me even more self-conscious! I managed to explain that I was just eager to get started and wanted to make a good first impression by staying calm but focused. I probably wasn't smiling enough or looked at the floor too much.

It can be strange being put on the spot in front of important people, and chatting about yourself. If you are nervous, get some practice in. Practice in the mirror at home. Practice with a friend, or practice talking to someone who is a stranger. Maybe in a café whilst talking to someone in the queue, out for a walk, or in the supermarket, simple as that. It will just get you a little bit more used to chatting about yourself whilst asking questions back as well. Remember, you are at an interview really just to prove you are the person shown on the CV, so be open, honest, and engaging. This is likely the start of a professional friendship, so being positive is pretty key. In essence, it really is just a chat.

Key points:

- Writing a CV is not difficult; keep it clear, relevant and informative.

- Combine and compliment your various documents.

- A small amount of quality, or a large amount of inconsistency?

- An interview is a conversation. Just have a chat.

1.2.2 A job and career to be enjoyed not endured.

Everyone has worries, big or small, even after just a few months in the industry. There will be plenty more to deal with as your career progresses and your responsibilities get broader, so it's important to enjoy the stress-free years in your early career.

Remember, it is just a building, enjoy it

A good piece of project advice I relied on, that came from a project director, was to remember that your project work is just another building. My project at the time was facing some uncertainties, so maybe he could sense I was a bit unsure of what was happening, and that it may have been worrying me. What you are working on always seems so important, but it really is just a building. There are billions of them in the world, some getting built right now, some getting torn down, some getting designed, and many getting redesigned. Your project is just another project in the world. It is probably the centre of all your efforts, you might be worried about deadlines, and you need to work your socks off at times, but all projects have twists and turns, problems, delays, and cost overruns. It will probably get built in the end, whether there are arguments or not, so embrace any anxiety as a learning experience.

Overall, my advice is to avoid taking everything too much to heart and wasting energy on worrying. You have got a long career ahead of you, plenty of interesting and hopefully enjoyable buildings to get stuck into, so worrying is not healthy for yourself or your company. Certainly, at an early age, you should not be loaded with the sort of responsibilities that are mentally affecting your well-being.

If anxiety is causing a constant impact on your professional or personal life, it is definitely time to seek someone to chat to. Identify problems early, because they might be easily solved by your colleagues or manager, so don't go further down the rabbit hole. A negative spiral can start if you don't approach your difficulties and take that step back. Knowing when things are getting out of hand is quite a perceptive skill. It is not my personal area of expertise by any means, but I have seen plenty of colleagues sick with worry about projects or deadlines, as we all have been. Having conversations earlier to approach it head-on, would have made a big difference to them. I have seen tears in the office plenty of times, and it has often just come down to unrealistic workloads.

Try not to 'waste' any of your working life, knowing you should ask for help but not wanting to. It can be daunting but it's an important step to take. Plenty of people discuss difficult issues at work without actually revealing that it's them having the problem, just so that they can gauge their colleagues' reactions and suggestions. It is important to ask others about their worries too. It builds trust and inclusivity. Keep it more secret between close friends if you need to, but don't tackle these things alone if there is a nagging feeling that it is more serious. There are good charities, groups, and support networks in place, such as the 'Architects Benevolent Society' in the UK. You should start that conversation with them, even if it does not develop into further contact. And of course, I am happy to be contacted if you would like to discuss any worries.

Remember, it is just a job, enjoy it

Your career will take a winding path. From my

experience, working in your early 20s should be almost 100% enjoyable. Working hard, learning, being invigorated by the world of work, earning your own living, but never getting too overworked that you become put off. Into your late 20s, with a few more years of experience, there will be harder times and more responsibility. Then by your early 30s, perhaps you will have forged a good niche for your skills, been involved in some exciting projects, and had a variety of industry experiences. Later than that into your 40s, there's probably going to be lots of things that you have to lead on or take control of outside of project work, so stay as happy as you can, for as long as possible. It's a marathon, not a sprint, in the architectural world.

As mentioned earlier, I have always felt great love and appreciation for architecture as an interest and hobby, not just employment. So, if professional life is causing some frustration, then the wider architectural world and building news can take my mind off it. You might only enjoy the day-to-day CAD work, the office environment, and project progression, without wanting to take any notice of your surroundings or buildings. Some colleagues you will meet may not even like architecture at all, they are just employed for their software skills. But for me, having a passion for looking at and researching other amazing buildings around the city or world, and having this interest alongside my career, was a good mental 'rest' from the professional mindset. It is good to distance yourself mentally and physically in whichever means you need.

1.2.3 Experiencing negatives, problems, and change

In early career years, you might be feeling way out of your depth. You will not be expected to set the world ablaze in your first job, so don't worry if you need some adjustment time early on. Simple things like a can-do attitude and an appetite to improve yourself are very valuable to the company. If your software skills and productivity are still developing, then bringing other benefits to the team is still useful. There will probably be a few stressful Friday deadlines and late nights, you will have good and bad days, but it is all part of the journey. For the most part, the team ethic in architecture offices has always been pretty positive in my experience, and you will meet lots of great people. The key is to communicate if there is something that you need to get better at. In a few years' time when you are no longer the junior staff member, I hope that you would look out for and encourage younger colleagues, when they have some tough adjustments to make. Be proactive about getting better and showing that you have that attitude to progress.

Confront problems carefully and logically

I had a trusted theory when trying to analyse if something was becoming a problem in my career and how I should improve it. I split it into chunks of time. If something was nagging in my job for a few weeks, I needed to get my head down, be positive, and get on with it, trusting that the issue will improve. If it was nagging me for over a month, I would probably need to approach my manager, mentor, or more senior colleague, to let them know what's on my mind and find some ways to change it or discuss it. If this same problem is persisting for more than two months, then I definitely had to take some action and establish a clear path ahead to put it right. It's a tough balance to know and decide when something is really hurting you, or whether it is just a tough few weeks at work, which everyone goes through. Don't carry problems for too long, it's a waste of your talent.

Analysing the big issues and how to sail through them is an important skill to possess. One of your colleagues in the office will likely be going through some issues in the background as well, so you will not be alone. Try to patiently understand how serious your problem really is, because nobody will have any idea about it unless you calmly and professionally share your thoughts. Bottling up some silent anger is not going to solve it, and might show through in your office personality. I have, unfortunately, come across several colleagues who seemed to operate on a level of anger nearly all the time. They seemed agitated and short-tempered as a standard. Seeing two colleagues potentially on a crash course can be very uncomfortable for everyone, so make sure that isn't you.

Airing grievances in the right way

I have 3 examples. Firstly, being involved in company Revit training. This was when the software was fairly new, and few colleagues were attending some in-house training. I felt I had been left out for some reason, and therefore, after about three or four weeks I realised it was bugging me slightly. So, I sent a polite email to my manager, asking whether I could be involved, because whenever the company migration to Revit had been mentioned before, I instantly put my hand up saying I would like to learn. After a couple more weeks, I realised this was making me a bit frustrated and I had not yet received a reply, so I asked my manager in person, and he revealed it was just a matter of timing with my current project commitments that he really wanted my skills for. I was soon put onto the training regime once my project work had slowed, and the problem was solved. A few months later, my skills had progressed well, and I started the journey of learning Revit. I am glad I did not get too disruptive when asking about it.

Secondly, which seems really funny looking back at it now, I had a small gripe about 'Friday drinks' in the office. On the last Friday of every month, the whole office (just over 100 people) was invited to the kitchen space to have some refreshments, snacks, and chat from 4:30pm onwards. There was a pool table right there too. Now, I certainly loved the social side of the office and would love a cold beer and some crisps to round off the day. But on some occasions, when I was still working really hard on a Friday deadline, having most of the office just meters from my desk with all the chatter, laughter, and noise that would inevitably come from people celebrating the end of their week, I became quite distracted and agitated whilst trying to concentrate on these important drawings. I thought this was manageable for a couple of months but then had to send an email to the finance director saying, again, very politely, that I really appreciated the company attitude of putting on free drinks and snacks, but I am working hard on drawings which directly contribute to the company meeting deadlines and making money. Hence it is quite counterproductive to have most of the office right on your shoulder basically having a party. Maybe the entertainment could start in one of the meeting rooms downstairs first? Therefore, you are not missing out on the fun if you are still glued to the desk frantically arranging drawings. Sure enough, the finance director understood my position and arranged the 'early finishers' to go downstairs first, then once 6pm had come, it would be more reasonable to have a noisier office space.

Before each instance, I felt slightly worried about getting frustrated in a professional environment. But a calm attitude to point out a problem, and suggest constructive ways to change it, gave a far better outcome.

Thirdly, and far more recently, I was amazed to see a company that still had a 'first come first served' attitude on handing out free office supplies or gifts to staff. In this case, it was a laptop, some other computer hardware, and occasionally flowers or snacks, sent in by suppliers or clients that would only go to waste over the weekend. It is ideal to put these to good use for staff to take home, but to award the person who could run fastest to the reception desk to grab it, seemed a bad method. What about those who worked on the floor below? They would never have the chance to see the email and rush up the stairs to grab it. What if they were on a vitally important phone call, but could really do with a laptop at home for their children's school learning? What if there was a disabled employee using a wheelchair who would like some of the freebies? Would someone else run past them and pick it up first? It was painfully obvious to me that some people would not have the chance to benefit, so I sent a slightly spiky email pointing this out. Gladly the policy was soon amended, and an office ballot system was set up to put your name forward if you are interested in any of those items. The company then had a Friday afternoon prize draw where a new winner can get the benefit each time.

Productivity challenges and working from home

Trudging into the office every day, every week, month

after month, can be pretty draining, and you need the weekends to recharge and be ready to go again on Monday morning. That sort of cycle will not really change, but the fact so many employees will now work from home due to the Covid-19 pandemic is a massive change. Depending on your commute time, the number of hours saved per week is huge. In other industries, employees have been allowed to work from home for a number of years, especially if the work is self-sufficient, and it helps to concentrate and avoid distractions. This was never really common in architecture, but that had to change recently.

The enforced working from home could be quite a disaster if it continues. For example, I was used to having a large desk space to expand drawings and spread-out various sketches as required by my tasks. The advantage of having your team sitting close together for quick questions, discussing project changes, and generally sharing information throughout the day was a massive benefit. I found the ongoing project chit-chat amazingly beneficial. Hearing the project architect on phone calls, knowing how other parts of the building are being designed which might affect my drawings, or seeing other team members go off for meetings or discuss dates and timelines was helpful. Then of course the informal tea breaks or lunchtime walks would be great for team spirit. This has really disappeared temporarily during the pandemic, and no amount of improved video calling software will ever change that.

There is not the same creativity and freedom of design thinking when working from your own home. Further bad news is that younger staff will be missing their mentoring and development time when they are no longer surrounded by older and more experienced colleagues.

Mentoring and development will have to come from more rigid, organised check-in sessions, so it misses those organic and casual discussions that really help continual learning. Hopefully, the industry will react to this and change will be forthcoming. There might also be a bit of responsibility on you, to push for self-development and ask your company what their policy is on this.

But with change comes opportunity

From the design side, be aware of the tangible impact from these sorts of changes. The industry often goes through patterns and trends, but these can be accelerated by events or sudden improvements in technology. Ultimately, the pandemic caused a massive increase in need for flexible home-working space.

Taking residential apartments and domestic house building, for example, layouts and regulation requirements had become pretty rigid and hardly changed through my professional career. Apartment layouts were restricted to a small entrance area, kitchen, and dining room, probably combined, with an open plan living room, utility / laundry space, then 1, 2, or 3 bedrooms with a couple of bathrooms. There was not much need for anything else, and the configuration had been done so many times, that it could not get much more efficient in terms of floor space or access to the natural light for window placement. However, the need for a work-from-home space means that the previously regimented square footage and layout of residential plans must adapt and improve, far quicker than when changes previously occurred. There will be a big push for small study areas, nooks or corners, tiny workrooms, or perhaps an attempt to add designated moveable furniture items to save space and allow a working from home option. It may only need a small notch in a room to comfortably allow a desk and chair, but the space must be of meaningful size to be designated for this purpose.

Directly as a result of the pandemic, that domestic design template has to change. It is not acceptable to shoehorn a desk and chair within centimetres of your bed corner, as many people have temporarily done, directly impacting how you arrange your home. Companies and employees will need to agree on a minimum, healthy, or acceptable workspace area. This will also directly impact furniture design, whereby fold-down or moveable desks / chair arrangements will be hugely popular. Change as a general concept often happens as a result of something else. It is a reaction to something. Hence this design change being a direct reaction to the virus, trying to stay away from people and the work from home increases. It is a necessity that has been created by an event and will push innovation.

The whole scenario is still quite up in the air right now, although I think gradually companies will want their staff back to the office as much as possible. It is problematic to have no physical separation between work life and home because your environment does not change. Commuting was actually a buffer of time to divide them. You psychologically need to break away from a location and move somewhere else completely to detach from work, to enjoy your personal evening or family time, but that is more difficult if you are not actually going anywhere. A direct impact of that will be to at least pack away your work items fully, into foldable, hidden, or separated furniture arrangements, so your evening and weekend house becomes quite different to the work layout. The impact on interior design is massive and is something you can think about in terms of future attitudes to residential design.

Be adaptable and flexible to change

Online meeting rooms will never be as good as face to face, in my opinion. The necessity of going to a meeting at another company office has changed dramatically. If you are meeting someone from another company who lives 100 meters from your house, but your official offices are ten miles away in the city centre, would you really bother both travelling that journey? What if the journey needs public transport connections as well as your trip to the station? It seems unnecessary to do that now. A logical solution is to hold that meeting in a local café or restaurant, but with limited space to spread drawings, or discuss confidential things in private. Would you consider hosting the meeting at your house? Or invite yourself to their house? It is a very odd possibility looking forward, but why not? I would not like to personally, but I bet it has happened somewhere over the past year because of the pandemic.

It is another very bizarre change to the industry, and not something I like the sound of, so hypothetically, how will design or travel solve this issue? I guess the 'virtual' experience will have to get better. Cafés and restaurants are already hosting far more business meetings than they used to and might actually be designing for that as a revenue stream.

Blurring that line between going into a building to represent your company, and doing so in casual public places, has interesting ramifications. Representing your company whilst sitting in your dining room, holding an important meeting with your children playing in the next room, is a very confusing result of all this, and I don't really think it will last. It's good to hypothesize about what architecture and design have to deal with, and what it has to adapt to. I am sure something else will eventuate in the coming years to change things again. Discussing this sort of thing with your colleagues will help you to understand the broad range of interpretations, and how a bunch of architecture professionals will all produce different ways to tackle issues like this.

There are always lots of changes happening in the industry, so it is good to be aware of them early on. Whether politically, financially, or socially driven, the world and its economies change quickly now, and it definitely affects the construction industry, so appreciating how it all links together is great to study. Particularly the last year has been far more isolated for many of us, but if you can somehow turn that into an opportunity to learn, acquire knowledge, and future proof your career, instead of stepping back on your ambitions and enthusiasm, you will be progressing continuously.

Key points:

• Work isn't always fun, so expect difficulties, but prepare remedies.

• Feel empowered to voice your problems and suggestions, but in the right way.

• Innovation comes from change, and design is innovation; understand the links.

1.2.4 Office folk - the good, bad, and the ugly.

A few years into your career, after experiencing typical office environments and navigating the stresses and strains of working life, it is good to take lessons from all of it. In the vast majority of projects, if the team works well together, the building will be a success. If the team ethic is lacking, there will be negativity, disagreements, and possible delays. That's within your own office team, as well as the consultants or clients involved. In this commercialized, and generally capitalist world (a big statement I know, but not to be expanded upon here), there are strong personalities, strong opinions, power struggles, moods, money, business efficiency and of course profits at stake. Try to keep in touch with what is happening day to day in your project, concerning both the company and the people.

Make no mistake, businesses try to and need to make money. The ongoing success of the business and the need for winning new projects is luckily a responsibility much higher up the chain than your early position requires. However, it is good to understand the basics and appreciate what everyone else is working on.

I will talk about mentoring a little bit more in subsequent sections, but it is something that I have enjoyed for a few years, and will continue with. I had a few mentors who did not really know they were mentors to me, but were very influential in terms of my learning. I think it is crucial to find someone to rely on and look up to. But also, to observe their reactions and behaviour in various situations, see how they apply their skills, and watch their career progress.

Understanding people, like your friends or family

You will meet some odd folk in your architectural journey. There will be a bit of everything. Loud, quiet, funny, annoying, rude, frightening, friendly, and childish. Prepare for it all, and gradually, you will need to read the room, decide who to rely on, and who to be a little bit careful of.

Depending on where you work, what size of company, and then simply what the personalities are like in your office, there will always be clashes. Human beings are generally good at working as a team. We are typically good at organising companies for group benefit. But be very sure that we are competitive too, and will always have characters who want to be the best at the expense of others. Some people will project themselves as superior, even when they are clearly not, and might want to push everyone else around, to feel like they are the best and dominating others. Soon, you will be able to see within your company, who is the quiet one, who is the loud one, who takes time to speak and is always right, who shoots early and is often wrong, who is the organiser, who is the crazy thinker, who is fun but perhaps annoying, etc. Human beings will always eventually disagree, and the extent or outcome of this disagreement is the crucial bit. The speed of resolution decides whether overall progress is made or not.

Everyone has their good and bad days, often with underlying arguments going on in the background. There is always a lot going on under the radar; some will be desperately looking for a promotion, some will have an ongoing gripe about the company, some will want a pay rise, some are completely bored with work, and some are just about to hand in their notice; there is probably some new staff arriving in just a few weeks. You will not always notice it, but the tangled web of human nature plays out in offices, where people want control, people want money, people want things done their own way, so it depends on how the various personalities are controlled to determine whether you see these things or not. There will be little arguments, scandals, or secrets that occasionally come out, but take it in your stride and concentrate on developing yourself and progressing. All the above is probably true of any industry, but for the most part, architectural folk are pretty genuine, intelligent, and should be good company.

To summarise this point, consider, and eventually, find out what sort of person you want to be in the office. What personality do you want to project out? It might not exactly be the personality you are at home. That's fine because the two environments are very different. Whatever personalities you see in the office, could be vastly different to their home version. Anyone could be dealing with tough domestic, financial, or health challenges that you don't know about. So, work on making good, strong relationships with colleagues who could help you in the future.

There were many colleagues I remember who, whilst not being friends with them outside of work at all, were great friends in the office, and we found common ground to chat about anything. This will make you feel more secure in the job, and have even more resources of the human kind, to learn from.

Key points:

- Office personalities are a mixed bag, be aware of colleagues' various circumstances.

- The most unpredictable, disruptive part of projects, are probably the people.

- What's your office 'personality'? Decide the image you want to project.

1.2.5 Choosing a company to work for

Immediately after university, or in the summers in between, your options of work might be limited geographically. Of course, in big cities, there are so many to choose from, but loosely planning where you would like to go even at an early stage is useful. There are big differences between how small and large companies operate, and how they can define your career.

Make a list or comparison

When deciding which companies to apply to, be prepared to be overwhelmed with choices. Your first task is to actually narrow it down. Initially, you may not care who you work for, in which case applying relentlessly and blindly to any local company may work. However, to be more thoughtful about your career path, your preferences can be made by location, size of company, reputation, history of work, typology of work, pay level, projects currently on the table, their attitude to people, approach to develop young staff, employees you already know, atmosphere of the office, type of work they have available for you, etc., there could be many more parameters to help you choose.

In the current age of working from home, this does give you vast options to approach companies from anywhere in the world, and conducting the entire application process online. But on the assumption that you would want to meet your colleagues and work in your town or city, you could consider making a list of nearby companies. In the past, when making such decisions myself, I have found it useful to make a chart, to rate each company out of 10, on a number of factors similar to those listed above.

For example, do the company's projects excite me? What role will I have there? Is it a short-term role or could I be employed here for years to come? How easy would my commute be? Is the office in a nice area of town? Any decent spots for a lunchtime walk? Are there enough people in the office make it interesting and stimulating? Bear in mind, an office of just five people could be quite intense and you would perhaps overhear everyone else's conversations in the office, but then again, with minimal people, you would have lots of very hands-on experiences, learning closely from colleagues. Would a company of hundreds of people leave you a bit overawed and lost? They might have good social outings, but it might feel a bit too corporate. Progression opportunities could be good in both cases.

In a big company, there could be training opportunities, business avenues to explore, and lots of ways in which your skills can be developed and improved, but then in a small company, you could get good exposure to your projects, so it would be easy to step up with promotion because there might be nobody else you are competing with. As you can see there is quite a lot to think about.

Wages on offer will probably be a consideration, although it is not always best to assume the higher wage is a better option. As long as the company is paying you a fair and comparable wage for the moment, that's what is most important before you start thinking of pay rises. At any age, it is a difficult decision to judge how things will work out; hence, your list of comparisons show what the 'total score' is for each company. I used that to decide two of my employer choices.

Another consideration, is how your CV might look in a few years' time? What will you be able to say about your time at this company? Have the projects been interesting, exciting, and educational? Perhaps they have projects only at certain stages, whereby you would be heavily involved in only concept designs, or executing onsite projects? There is a massive difference in the skills you need at opposite ends of the projects, so be aware that concept drawings versus construction drawings give you vastly different skills. This first step might define what you can do for the next few years.

Then there is the reputation and status of the company. Are they globally known? Are they developing fast? Do they only design certain typologies? Do they rely on a small number of reliable, repeat clients? Solely working on hotel or residential blocks could be quite repetitive and boring, but then you would get consistent experience in this typology and build up some good expertise to specialise in.

Next, will there be opportunities to travel in the job? Any international projects? At least you would want some site visit opportunities to see the results, or you may like to get to know a region very well by sticking to local work, and building a portfolio of your architectural activity consistently in one town.

Knowing about the culture of a company becomes extremely important. You would probably want a company that really invests in and looks after their staff, perhaps helping target new qualifications, or providing enough training to improve skills. Then, of course, the social side of the office, with initiatives or sports or clubs. Are there enough people in the company who are of similar age? Similar interests? A group you can easily identify with and feel supported by would be ideal.

Then the potentially dreaded scenario, who you are directly working with? What is your boss like? Everyone has heard stories of terrible bosses, but it really can make or break things. Early on, you need support, guidance, enjoyment, a bit of slack, time, and patience from your managers. Someone who can remember what it is like being young and daunted by their first few years. Do you want a boss who will push you really hard but makes you rapidly improve in your career? Or someone willing to guide you, but ultimately lets you just settle into the industry gently in your first few years?

Specialisms and typologies

One additional thing to point out, is that many architects concentrate only on certain typologies, work primarily in certain locations, or concentrate on certain stages of projects. For example, a company might refuse to chase projects of certain typologies if they do not have those specific skills in the office. If a client wants a new hospital, but the company and employees have no hospital experience, it would be risky to take on that project.

Primary schools or airports would be further examples of where prior experience would be extremely beneficial. Clients would, in reality, choose or know which companies have the relevant experience for their brief, so would be taking a risk themselves if they were not employing an architect with the requisite knowledge to do the job well.

The companies I first worked for, both specialised almost solely in residential, commercial and hospitality projects, because that was where their experience lay, and they knew they could execute those projects effectively. Similarly, some architects position themselves specifically as concept architects, whereas the term 'executive architect' in the UK, refers to a company who takes on that concept design, and is more suited to the details, coordination and regulation matters. Therefore, getting the right exposure to typologies, stages and deliverables is important to decide, because it affects your future opportunities.

Setting some general goals

Looking back on my 16 years of employment experience, I never planned my career in the way it has ended up. At several points, I had no idea what was next and probably should have set some goals in my late 20s.

To split it into a few separate stages, my first intention after university was simply to find any job to get into the world of work, which was understandable but maybe a bit rushed. I saw and answered an advert for a stadium refurbishment job in London, which I jumped at, despite it being a slightly arduous journey out of London each day to the office. It was a great project, with good bonuses, and colleagues who I really liked working with. There was good progression opportunities and great pay. But the long commute was tiring, hence, not having much evening time to myself was tough. Additionally, the company did mostly residential work, so I may have felt stifled after a few more years.

My next move was solely intending to work in the middle of London. I went to a slightly larger firm, to enjoy the overall lifestyle and variety of projects, now that I had a good couple of years of grounding. After several years of developing well at that company, my horizons broadened and the opportunity to go abroad came up, from chasing some contacts on LinkedIn. I knew others who had taken the same jump to work abroad, so I was interested in anywhere that would take me, just to get set up. It was an experimental time, and I initially thought I would be back in London after a couple of years, but it turned into a very enjoyable and educational move. During nearly five years I saw all manner of projects, some that went well and some that went horribly wrong. Finally, my most recent relocation to Melbourne came about from keeping in touch with old contacts in the Middle East, through some casual messages every few months. Right now, I have fairly rigid plans for the next four or five years but things could change completely again after that.

It is not much effort to set some broad targets for yourself, which will contribute to shaping a great career. From a young architecture professional's point of view, I would advise that your short-term plan (up to 1 year ahead) should be fairly well set, secure and reliable, so you know where you will be and that you are learning and developing. The medium-term (perhaps 1 – 3 years ahead) could be wildly open, take you anywhere in the world, and encourage broad thinking about your entire career development or specialisms and typologies you like. Then long term (five years plus) should be more tangible and focused to identify bigger life targets that may not eventuate anytime soon, but act like overall guidance. That will ensure that in seven or eight years' time, you have got some really good progress in your back pocket to set you up for the next long-term goals. Write these down in your notebook or on a memo page on your phone, somewhere that you will see regularly, and remind yourself of what you are aiming for.

Key points:

• Try a chart or scoring system to choose companies to apply for, they're not all great.

• This first step in your career can be quite defining, do not rush it.

• Short, medium, and long-term goals can help to give you some balance.

1.3 CURRENT INDUSTRY SKILLS

1.3.1 Architecture as a hobby.

1.3.2 Sketching skills, the humble pencil.

1.3.3 Confront construction detailing.

1.3.4 Embrace site work and visual perception.

1.3.5 Utilising endless resources.

1.3.6 Software skills and self-improvement

1.3.1 Architecture as a hobby

I think it is important to really love this subject. The industry can certainly be frustrating and overwhelming enough that unless you have a deep desire and enjoyment of architecture, it might push you too hard and too far over several years. Your desire for it will certainly be challenged over the years. It is a never-ending job and journey, so to stick with it through thick and thin is quite a dedication to shaping the built environment.

Keep the bigger picture in mind, and remember that you are doing a service to people, and a duty to society that not many people get to do. Generally, I think architecture will need to be part of your life as a hobby as well as your job. Or certainly, it will help to have that wider appreciation. It is commonly said that if you are going to spend upwards of 40 hours a week in employment, you might as well be doing something you enjoy.

It is a brilliant time to be involved in architecture. The possibilities have gone absolutely through the roof in the past 10 or 15 years. It is a simple but respected subject in terms of historical reputation and standing. It is a trusted, high level, impressive, and overall worthwhile subject. But it has become really, really cool in my lifetime.

First of all, the shapes and futuristic schemes mostly made famous by the likes of Zaha Hadid or Bjarke Ingels have really stretched the design approach to be a vibrant, visual, organic object, instead of just a building. In my upbringing, buildings were mostly block-shaped, generally at right angles, all from concrete, brick, glass, or steel, and were just a place you go in order to do something or buy something. To understand and value them on a different level is a special feeling.

I cannot really pinpoint where the change was for architecture becoming cool, but perhaps very loosely, you can say that the combination of technological improvements along with the internet exchanging so many ideas and concepts, has led to an amazingly eclectic couple of decades, where anything goes. As long as the design is extremely attention-grabbing, the client will want their building to make headlines around the world, sometimes regardless of how it is built or how it performs. That visual headline is so important, and design concepts have followed that mantra, that the crazier the shape, the better. Marketing is so much more powerful in architecture now, that a building needs to have the wow factor above the logical or more standardized approach.

Architecture is an open, democratic subject

Everyone can try their hand at architecture now. TV programmes showing so many self-builds of brilliant domestic houses are allowing people with nearly zero architecture experience to design their own house and have it refined by an architecture professional. The world of design is much more accessible now, through websites, magazines, product mailing lists, and even social groups. There are so many areas of the industry you can fit into now, and there are so many more ideas being brought to the table.

Perhaps the difference now is that architectural education and expression has been allowed to run wild. There is more ability to gain knowledge of buildings from any random corner of the world, with more media sites to present them and share ideas about. In my youth, I would have had to go to my local library to find architecture books to educate myself about even just a handful of buildings. But now I can blitz through hundreds of images in just a few minutes with the most unusual and obscure Google search.

The breadth of ideas has influenced young architects' minds and pushed their imaginations to go further. Computer game simulations now are far better than anything in my youth. They are more like a secondary version of life. But those fictitious worlds still need designing. Things like SimCity and Minecraft are incredibly simple, but popular concepts for entertainment.

A few years ago, I was really keen to work on designing film sets or theme parks, and that section of the industry is booming now. Anything is possible, and fresh ideas are valuable, so you would not ever be squeezed out of the industry by the older, more experienced people as perhaps would have happened before. Ideas or designs from younger generations get more publicity and limelight now, so the traditional trusted methods of design or construction can be challenged easier. There are so many factors at play.

Pure skills and experience overtake qualifications

Inclusion and accessibility to entry level jobs are so much better as well. Authentic qualifications do not seem as essential now. The vast number of qualifications in the architecture subject, generally, allow many routes into work. I am a good example of that, having been temporarily employed as a project architect on a number of occasions, despite being qualified as an architectural technologist. Hence this book was nearly called 'The Story of a Failed Architect.' Historically in the UK, you had to be quite rigidly qualified as an architect to take that role. The title of being an 'architect' is still rightly protected. However, after only about 6 years of professional experience post-graduation, my experience, knowledge, and office manner allowed me to step into job runner roles, albeit temporarily.

Where I have seen that in reality, is companies are holding internal design competitions. This was originally reserved for qualified professionals only. The past three companies I have worked for, allow literally anyone in the company to throw forward their concepts and ideas with fun, internal design competitions, and the project gets more serious as it progresses. More general design knowledge can apply to architecture now. Simply by showing the process of satisfying a need with a solution constitutes the design process. Architecture has increased and diversified as a subject, so maybe that means there is

119

even more to understand, more to investigate, so you can pick and choose where you want to be involved.

My three favourite parts of the architecture industry

There are three particular areas that I find constantly exciting and stimulating about the industry; they are future design, historical architecture and construction detailing.

How we are transitioning our building techniques like the modular approach, biomimicry, or moving buildings are fascinating future design progressions. Architecture leads and influences lifestyles, and the methods used can do so as well. I find it a captivating story to follow. Inevitably our construction style and the prevalent aesthetic of architecture does go in cycles and waves, but biomimicry and adjustable moving buildings would never have been on the radar in previous generations. I was fascinated by the recent intentions to erect demountable football stadiums to reuse at world cups, or to have a moveable pitch effectively on a barge, boat, or platform, which can move around the harbour or marina sites in the Middle East. They are superb, visionary, and logical thinking. These sorts of challenges get me excited about the future and how we can all contribute to these seemingly unbelievable designs.

Away from my employment demands over the years, I have always been interested in learning more about the history of architecture and studying old heritage buildings. I still watch those YouTube documentary videos of old classical buildings, long lost temples, or the evolution of cities and how original buildings still stand today. I found history to be an amazing (and again, never-ending) subject to learn from. I was lucky enough to work on several historical schemes, in some incredible heritage-protected parts of London. It feels like you are involved in a little slice of history and playing your part in the story of globally known locations. There are so many incredible old buildings that act as a view into the local history or an example of that society years ago. Buildings now are generally designed for an approximate 60–80-year shelf life. Why is it so short? So many historical buildings are still standing many, many hundreds of years later. Have we regressed in our capabilities of designing and constructing long-lasting buildings?

Finally, the visual clarity of detailing really caught my imagination from an early age. Perhaps developing from my enjoyment of simple building block toys and construction challenges as a child, then even messing around with Lego, Meccano, and woodwork, from there blossomed a keen interest in studying detailed construction drawings to get that orthographic view of what a building joint looks like when you take a cut through it. It has been the most influential part of my career too. Pretty quickly I was hooked into investigating and solving detailing issues, enjoying the puzzle-like nature of the junctions, and wanting that base-level knowledge of construction that lots of professionals do not have. This skill is discussed more in the next section.

And some dislikes too

Conversely, there are a few things I have never been keen on. I was never too desperate to undertake the job runner role in previous companies. There will often be the opportunity for you to fill in on certain duties whilst other colleagues are away, but once I had entered the world of work after university, I realised I did not want to return to study for my diploma. I could quickly see project architects spending more of the day on Microsoft Outlook, than detailing or designing the building fundamentals. Project architects seemed to be moving more into an organizational role, away from the real business of drawing and understanding how the building is going to work for its occupants.

The ongoing embrace of new software always left me a bit cold too. I was excited to learn software once it was up and running, instead of trying out new experimental versions. Especially now that there are so many to learn, it is probably good advice to find out what software companies are using before concentrating your skills on one of them. In terms of favoured typologies, after just a few years in practice, I felt quite bored with residential projects and residential towers. There are some exciting parts to the initial design and, of course, high-rise can be fascinating. But with the generally low London skyline, I was probably influenced by the standardization of layouts and relentless pursuit of increasing square footage, all to generate more millions for a wealthy client. It left me feeling a bit stifled. It seemed a lot of effort for little reward.

There was not a huge amount of imagination left in apartment design, because of the restrictive nature of regulations, and building owners calling the shots. After just a few months of experience, you might find yourself liking and disliking different parts of the industry, but be aware, they could easily change too.

Take the initiative, have a specialism

There is so much to educate yourself about, that, in my opinion, there is no excuse not to dive into some specifics and become an expert in the field that you want to. Every day you should be scouring websites, reading articles, studying interesting new products, skimming through architecture images online, and generally immersing yourself in the subject. Don't think too much about project work, but more the enjoyment and mental stimulation of what the design world can show you and what buildings say to you.

Key points:

• Would you be better at your job if it's a passion and hobby too?

• Spend time talking about architecture or jumping into online forums.

• Know exactly what you can bring to the table, and be proud of it.

1.3.2 Sketching skills, the humble pencil.

You might frequently hear the line: "I'm terrible at drawing" around the office, but I never quite believe it. I think the reality is: "I've never given drawing enough time or effort, so I just assume I can't do it." It seems strange in a subject that is so reliant on visually representing something on paper, but I have worked with plenty of very talented architects who somehow make their sketches look really bad. Often never in proportion or near a decent scale, where often by the time you are finished, you have to politely ask, is that drawn in plan or section? People who can draw, are just making simple lines on a page. They are making intricately complicated and arranged lines in a certain order, but anyone else can do if they sit there next to them and draw exactly the same lines. Like playing the piano or making tiny delicate models, you are just training your hands and fingers to do the same that someone else does, in a very coordinated manner. Perhaps best to leave the "can't draw" people as they are, so it heightens the fact that you can.

Sketching, in my view, is hugely important for young architectural professionals. Firstly, it's a very useful and fun skill to have, but also very admired and quite rare. Using a pencil seems archaic now, but to research things like the 'golden triangle,' or the 'rule of thirds,' reminds you of the centuries-old theoretical laws of architecture and design. It is a bit of a break out feeling as well because such skills are not so useful in practice.

In reality, sketching is time consuming. Careful, perfect sketching will not always be hugely applicable in most office situations, and you will not get much time to do it properly in terms of the pressurized office environment. But there is something hugely enjoyable to me about a perfect pencil sketch. It is creative and evokes more than just artwork. I think any good architecture sketch can add to the building, and encourage you to think of the building differently beyond the angle of the sketch.

Not just a hobby but an applicable talent

You have probably used software, where the online model you have built, can be visually manipulated to give a 'sketchy'-like quality with the click of a button. Unfortunately, this kind of technology is taking over the abilities to sketch by hand. But try to find time at home to sketch as regularly as you can. A five minute sketch is still valuable because it might be the first five minutes of a ten hour long masterpiece. A sketchbook lying around near your sofa might be as effective for you as having a full drawing board. Whatever set up you think suits you best, just give it those first five minutes and keep it ticking along.

Unfortunately, as mentioned, it is not hugely useful in professional practice, but where it will become priceless is for quick drawings to represent details, in discussions with other team members. These common team gatherings always rely on a few sketches and instant visualisations to describe their point, which is really useful. Architects love to take a little idea (set off by someone else's work or a fleeting moment of design thinking), and then use it as their own.

There is inspiration everywhere for the next design. You might see sketches in company literature or marketing materials that retain that personal quality. If you can sketch well, and show it, people will walk by in the office and stop to comment. They'll be interested to see 'a dying art kept going.' Nobody walks past your desk and says 'oh what a lovely specification you've got, or lovely finishes schedule on Excel.' Keep those sketches going in your spare time if necessary, and continue it when you have a few minutes to spare. They may even be shown on marketing materials or websites, as was done in my first company to show off their employee's talents.

Key points:

- Practice sketching either briefly or at length.

- Quick sketching in 3D is vital for design team chats and detailing.

- Some of the world's most famous buildings can be sketched in a matter of seconds.

1.3.3 Confront construction detailing

Arguably far more useful in current architectural practice is construction detailing. Via sketching or project models, the more you can visualise details and use them during meetings or design chats, the better. If you can clearly show on paper what people are discussing but disagreeing about, you can really prove your worth. Software skills will be held above nearly all others, but the quick freehand drawing on notepads and mark-ups is vital. Hopefully, your company will have design competitions or an open forum on ideas, where you can emerge as a visual, creative, design orientated staff member.

Find your own way to visualise

Trying your hand at detailing leads to construction knowledge. It is like a kit of parts; a puzzle that you have to tessellate, and arrange into logical ordering. Conversely, construction knowledge leads to better detailing. I would definitely recommend targeting construction detailing for your professional development. Through university, I felt detailing was somewhat lost in the demoralizing maze of studying unnecessary physics, heat gains and structural stresses. But the Construction in Architecture module represented one of my best scores through the course, and that interest has continued all the way through my career.

For one assignment about construction technology, I visited a local building site to ask for a tour, to take pictures, and to be shown a few drawings. The experience made so much more sense from seeing it on a real project. The cogs were turning and it made a lot of sense knowing that if one thing was connected to the other, then from a 90-degree angle it would look like that, or from the top view like this, and then the side view like this, and so on.

Perhaps those skills are innate to a point, but that success probably gave me a bit of a boost to be able to assess buildings and know what has been constructed. Similar to those mental challenges or puzzle books for cognitive aptitude, to identify the one correctly represented shape out of four options, based on a certain view of it from a different angle. Those mind games can be great training.

Architecture is still building with blocks

To relate that to detailing, you can break it down into simple functions and principles of each building element. The building needs to stand up and create this span, so that heavy block can rest on that very sturdy column. That surface needs protection so we'll fix a cover over it, and then that needs to be kept warm so we'll throw insulation in there. This junction must deflect water away so you make gradients to drain the water in this direction. If you can carefully talk yourself through the principles of the detail, after a while it becomes very simple to see why buildings stand up and lock together in watertight and airtight boxes.

Studying heavily annotated details can look daunting, but to systematically go through it and see that each item is doing its own job, will all make sense. Getting the highlighter out to first establish the substrate (probably concrete or steel) and then colour the internal linings, and identifying the insulation is a good start. Use consistent colours each time you do this.

A very good analogy which you may have heard is that the human body is the equivalent of a building. The bones are like the structure, with the muscles, ligaments, and tendons being like fixings, brackets or bracing. That leaves the vessels, veins, and nerves to be the plumbing and electrics. Things all work together to hold each other up and connect in different ways. Which bit connects to which, which holds that in place, this protects that, and this bit holds that in the right way, so this can move in this direction because of the joint type. All that should make sense once you study it carefully.

Did the ancient Egyptians make construction details? Or the Romans, Aztecs, or any similar civilization of people thousands of years ago? The fact that many examples of their buildings are still here today, suggests that even if they did not draw out what they wanted, they certainly understood how it was going to go together and stay there. Here we are, thousands of years later, and there is so much dependence on hundreds of structural and architectural details we draw so that a group of builders can figure out how you want a building made.

Back in the ancient civilizations, there would have been a tight hierarchy of who was ordering who around, immeasurably different to today. But one thing that remains, is that knowledge can trump all others. If you can be the one to know and prove how buildings can be built, to achieve the visual outcome of the design, you will always be in demand in the industry.

Detailing is a necessary and rewarding skill

I wrote this quote for a CIAT conference presentation about my development in the industry, and I think it is still relevant to viewing what is important as an architecture professional:

During my university degree and first few years of employment, I developed a huge interest and ambition to learn, not only about the visual and aesthetic qualities of buildings and the environment, but also to explain the science and technology behind them. I want to be the person who can not only design and detail the building but also describe how and why it works in the way it does.

When I ventured into the industry, construction detailing was luckily hugely in demand. Looking back before that, in the post-war building boom in the UK particularly, it was quite haphazard, obviously quick, and done without relevant checks or verification. It was certainly not to a high standard. The backlash against that probably came into view in the 1960s and 70s, after some terrible apartment fires exposed poor building techniques. Gradually, building materials enabled better envelope design and improved air circulation. Buildings became a breathing animal, a 'machine for living in' (definitely a good quote to research), and a comfortable place to live and prosper. The demand for housing stock has always

129

been there, but the personalised nature of design has grown. In the historical towns of the UK, most of the population could walk into the adjacent terraced house and know it was the exact same layout in their house. You knew what 90% of your neighbour's houses were like inside.

Improved building quality is often down to legislation and liability; hence construction details became far more important than previously. So, perhaps I joined the industry at a good time in which detailing was being understood more and was certainly far more important than it had been before, from an insurance and therefore, financial point of view. Upon exiting university, the slightly more senior roles that I was looking at, for example, in technical detailing or a draughtsman role, were pretty much on a par with a 'Part 3 qualified Architect.' Great news for me, and perhaps an extra impetus to be interested in detailing and to be the one who tackles it head-on.

Create your architectural identity

I badged myself in that way on my CV, talking as much as possible about detailing, UK Building Regulations, and understanding drawing packages. I was instantly at the forefront of documentation, organising all relevant views, drawing numbering and navigation around the set. A project architect can be the most underpaid in terms of the time and money spent in education.

In my London employment, I needed to specialise in something, so it gradually became detailing and product knowledge. I was always sure to ask the company technical group and learn as much as I could from them. I was a pest to them by asking lots of questions but trying to see their thought process and absorb their skills and the way they analysed details. In my UK years, I would read the Detail magazine all the time, go through the Building Design magazine on the commute, and use the Architects Journal every week to keep absorbing all the information I could. I was not necessarily understanding all of it, but just getting more and more comfortable with building design, so that within a few minutes I could understand all parts of the detail. Even if all the annotations of products are often scientific names or compounds being used, I knew roughly what was going on.

Presentation is of paramount importance on the construction details. Simple rules of alignment on drawings, getting the gridlines matching up so that you can read the head detail directly above the slab edge detail, directly above the sill or footing detail. Lucky for you now, Revit and ArchiCAD do this for you. It used to be easy to make mistakes, now I feel like a lot is already refined, with safety nets and reminders for what to check or finish. Alignment of annotations at the side of the drawing, then even punctuation and spelling mistakes would just take the edge off the quality. Every drawing you do should be so clear that a total novice can pick it up and know what is happening.

My director once told me, if you have a beautifully presented drawing, in terms of alignment, sensible ordering, use of the page, and rigid title blocks, you can often get away with a few detail omissions or mistakes. Construction details are more important than the amazing images of the building for the sales and marketing pages. Those details you produce are where the company can be sued, so your standards need to be high. My career position now is mostly thanks to an initial four or five years of continually grinding out general arrangement drawings, works packages and construction details.

Knowledge is power in construction

I think detailing is changing in terms of documentation output, but the 2D drawings as a submission form will be around for a few years yet. Software technology has enabled massive advances in what can be done with design and integration, creating brilliant 3D views, but the vast majority in the industry still operates on simpler details.

There are many priorities for you and it will take a few years, but construction experience is something I think you really do work for and get better at. It is not a subject that is easily overridden by young aspiring architects, so in that sense, anyone with sharp detailing skills is in a secure job. It is the graphical and software experts that must relentlessly adopt the new ideas and produce improved images. But by having construction knowledge, you will always be in demand, simply from detailing and knowing how buildings are put together.

Key points:

• Every detail is different and every product brings new learning possibilities.

• Use colour to understand detailing; each item is doing a specific job.

• Detailing is a safe haven and can't be automated, so knowledge is power.

1.3.4 Embrace site work and visual perception

Years ago, I devised a handy approach using my own anatomical measurements to define and confirm dimensions, shadow gaps, distances, heights, and clearances on various jobs. It was vitally useful at site inspections, conducting site reports, and knowing the standardized measurements that make up regulations. On some occasions, I was able to prove someone right or wrong by guaranteeing them that a measurement or distance was not to regulations or my detail drawings. Even now I know for sure that, for example, the width of the nail on my little finger is 10mm. From the end of my index finger to the knuckle is 100mm. My total handspan width is 220mm. And from the nobble on my elbow to the tip of my middle finger is 440mm. If I stand up completely straight, I am 1m and 94cm. With my hand stretched fully up into the air, that is a convenient 2.4m high, a very common ceiling height. Knowing exactly where your hip bone is in terms of door handle heights or surfaces would also be a good one to know if you don't have a tape measure to hand.

I used those dimension checks so often on-site visits and inspections. Some of these tricks helped me immensely, in having the confidence to spot and correct things according to the details. Clear lines and good proportions were the specialism of that current company. You will be well respected if you have a few of these little tricks up your sleeve when discussing the accuracy of drawings or installations.

I was always so inquisitive on-site, that I would take

such a close look at everything. I wanted to analyse and intensely think about how it is made or how it is fixed. Spending a few hours on-site was absolute bliss for me. I had my site safety induction, and could wander off by myself and take notes of the building finishes and compare them to all my drawings.

Those were extremely valuable years, to take my time, closely inspect the installations, and start to understand every building item and how they all interlink. I could then take all that knowledge and evidence from my site photos back to the office, confident that I was basing my reports on very accurate measurements of what I had just seen.

Getting into the technical details of installed products was a big learning curve for me and allowed me to feel very confident of my abilities. If you can arrange time on-site, grab it with both hands. All architectural qualifications should have some prerequisite time on a building site. It does not make sense that newly qualified architects have hardly ever spent any time actually seeing a building go up. It sounds like a professional chef who has never tasted the meals that they make.

Key points:

• Site work is probably the most educational aspect of the industry, grab it.

• Building your knowledge builds confidence, which builds your influence.

• Measure up your body, it will come in very handy.

1.3.5 Utilising endless resources

Unfortunately, there are no excuses for a lack of research in architecture. The resources are everywhere. On a daily basis, I am still searching or finding products, downloading online technical literature or BIM objects, and studying how the systems work. Take a look at all the materials, fixings, warranties, guarantees, sustainability credentials, raw materials, location of their manufacturing, etc. The technical drawings section will be easily found on most decent product websites. Then if that does not work for you, pick up the phone and ask them. It is easy to shy away from asking simple questions when you are young, but in barely a one minute conversation the company reps can answer your questions. You are much more likely to remember the answer because it is a personal conversation. This is a great way to get more comfortable in the industry. Start finding out how suppliers and manufacturers fit into the whole project life cycle. Glossing over details will not necessarily sink in, so give them a quick call and keep your inquisitiveness going.

The supplier companies will probably want to get you on their mailing list, which you don't have to agree to. They will possibly want to pepper you with marketing material and various offers, and would potentially give you freebies and invites to all sorts of events, days out, or treats. These companies are leaning on you to specify their product, so they want to treat you well.

It is helpful to expand your network and become a known professional around the industry. If suppliers convince you about their product, then you can suggest it to your team and get it specified in your project, if your client agrees to the cost. Seeing how this side of the industry operates is good to know, because labelling a system or product on your drawings, doesn't necessarily mean it will be in the final built project. Check out and ask your project director about value engineering.

Just a small improvement every day

A very useful website I used is 'designbuildingswiki.' It is quite a basic but clear way to look up definitions. Google pretty much throws up any result you could ever think of, so if you are not using search tools at least three times a day to look up all manner of terms, then you are probably not pushing hard enough. At my relatively good standard of architecture knowledge, I still use it around three or four times a day. Some items will not soak into your long-term memory, but if 50 or 60% of it sticks, then you will be improving every day. Having favourites on your web browser or phone is ideal for looking up the most trivial of things whenever you want. That deep construction knowledge is priceless and I fully recommend trying to absorb as much as possible. Make a list of terms you didn't know this week, so there is a challenge to tick them off by next week.

Key points:

• Detailing is difficult, but it's not difficult to start researching it.

• Take time to know how suppliers and manufacturers affect projects and costs.

1.3.6 Software skills and self-improvement

With all that building knowledge being absorbed every day, keep the bigger picture in mind of being able to produce the goods on paper. The vast majority of that will be done on software. The term 'standard detail' has been around for years, and it has taken a long time for companies to really adopt it to maximum efficiency.

Opportunities for efficiencies

Originally restricted to standard wall junctions or objects, by now the common details certainly should be widely utilised. Many companies would have already done 70% or 80% of the details on their current job. So, with increased connectivity and storage of data throughout the project, there are plenty of standard details that should not be started from scratch. There will always be some new details to enhance the design, but getting that software efficiency of reusing details will be a big part of your job. If your company does not have that set up yet, it is a massive opportunity for you to step in and control it. Arranging a library of commonly used details that can be easily accessed and applied to any other job going forward, ideally matched up with specification clauses, will be a huge time saver.

Suggesting training for continual improvement

The industry has lagged on really utilising technology, but I think it is mostly here now. If you can be a leader of that, and demonstrate its benefits, it will be an excellent feature of your skills. An easy way of looking at this is to put yourself at the head of the company. If some of your newest and youngest staff are actively thinking of new technology and improved strategies to deliver projects, it is a brilliant benefit to the company. The management will soon be looking to that person as someone who is in touch with modern methods, can be the inspiration for other staff, and can suggest genuine business improvements.

Courses, training, or internal resources should be available for your own development whilst at the company, so if there is no sign of these things, you can raise it with the managers as a way to improve knowledge and staff output. Each employee can be a better resource, and therefore, a better money maker. Keep in mind there will always be the costs vs benefits analysis from the management, but any company would love their staff to be rapidly improving without too much effort from the management level.

Understanding the most prevalent software in your location might be crucial to your development. Revit and ArchiCAD is pretty dominant, but you will need one expert level skill that the company can rely on you for, plus a couple of other programmes you know to an intermediate level to back that up. To take on further skills is always encouraged, but not at the expense of your core skills. This sort of thing will depend on the size of your company, with larger companies being a bit more likely to put on training courses because of the time and cost options. The 3D and virtual reality realms of building design are really bubbling up, so if anything, that is the place where you can teach yourself some skills and be able to at least advise your colleagues, and potentially help to implement it.

Key points:

- Take a lead on something; bring some expertise or critical thinking to the table.

- Find out the company approach to software efficiencies and how to use them.

- Keep an eye on the next step, what will your company use in 10 years' time?

1.4 COMMON BUILDING MATERIALS

The discussion and use of the word 'materiality,' and therefore, the understanding of materials and their place in architecture, is very common. Entire books are written about how powerful materiality can be in the final aesthetic. Clearly a concrete building, a timber building, or a steel building would give a very different feeling or visual impact to their design, directly because of the inherent materials qualities.

Opinions and tastes could be vastly different depending on who you are talking to, but that is part of the enjoyment of design. I still spend many hours flicking through those big coffee-table architecture books, usually showing incredible private house designs or the unseen architectural gems. Materials give an atmosphere to a building, similarly to the font, graphics, and colours choice giving a vibe to your CV that was discussed earlier. This is the magic of architecture and design, and it is a sight to behold when a designer really cracks it.

Below is a quick discussion about common materials and their application. Learning about materiality in architecture is a bit like taking up a musical instrument; quite easy to learn the theory and play a quick tune, but very difficult to master.

Stone.

Obviously a very natural material, and with many different types, layers, colours, and textures available. Stone is a fantastic building material in terms of earthiness, giving such a natural appearance, but also a hard, solid, and certainly traditional feeling. It can give a feeling of high quality and rarity, especially when using marble for example. Colours and strata arrangements can show amazing geological patterns. Stone has been used right from the very start of architectural history, so you will be able to find thousands of good examples online. The atmosphere created by seeing stone used well on buildings suggests age, but also durability, and permanence. The 'personality' of the stone finish will be the same in 2 weeks or 50 years, so I also find it very stable, reliable, and assured.

Stone is most commonly used as wall and floor tiles but also for interior decoration in worktops or tables. Cladding panels, external walls, or paving would use quite common stone panels with considerations for their density and therefore weight to be hung on the wall details. The size options are broad, many shapes can be accurately cut, or stone can be left natural when using authentic blocks or boulders. There is a huge range of stone quality and cost that you can choose from, usually depending on where it is quarried from.

Brick.

In a similar way to stone and rock, I like that brick gives the sense of human touch mixed with history. A crucial difference or advantage is the human scale of a traditional brick. It has that domestic feeling that it must have been placed by hand and not mass-produced. It has been manufactured to such an extent of options in recent years, that it has almost got a man-made quality, despite being made of clay of course. Brick was mostly sized and shaped to pretty exact dimensions, being 80x110x215mm, but now comes in many other sizes, shapes, and thicknesses or in panels called brick slips. Improved mass production facilities allowed companies to invent or develop many new patterns or dimensions based on designers pushing the boundaries.

Brick can be visually organised in terms of patterns and configuration to form texture and facades. It is very structured and linear, therefore, not as natural as stone would be, but it still conveys a sense of raw primal building but can look very labour intensive or simple. I used to be fascinated by the 'Brick Bulletin' website and magazine in the UK that featured many brilliant but simple brick designs. Take a look yourself.

Timber.

Certainly, a favourite building material, being so inherently natural, but in practice, it is commonly faked to significant effect using veneers and photographic application of timber grains. In a very similar way to stone and rock, timber gives a very honest, harmonious, and clean but rugged, natural style. It can be used in nearly any conceivable way in a building, like flooring, walls, cladding, furniture, worktops, homeware, roofing, doors, and joinery.

Cladding in timber is extremely common, in terms of boards and panels, often horizontally laid in planks on battens, but also vertically. Various finishes can and should be applied for both internal and external use, which often helps to display the beautiful grain patterns.

Something a bit different to search for is 'Japanese mechanical timber joints.' There are no chemicals used in the assembly or fixing. It is purely the angle and forces of the geometry, resulting in amazing balanced looking construction. I have seen recent notable news stories featuring the first timber building skyscraper, and a timber football stadium in the UK. Innovation always pushes the boundaries and timber has a long way to go on that. Certainly, bamboo should be in the same category.

Concrete.
This is a relatively new material and was a fantastic invention at the time. It is partly made from crushed rock, called aggregate, so in that sense, natural, but its process makes it very much a man-made material and extremely damaging to the environment because of its huge water usage and intensive method. It's not a material I dislike, because it can create a certain mood, whilst being quiet and introverted at the same time.

Through the 1960s and 70s, an entire movement called brutalism was inextricably linked to concrete because of its hard, harsh, emotionless, sterile, and often bland appearance. But it was used for those exact qualities to give a certain truth and monotony as well. It was deliberately used, and very successfully too, as a heavy and solid material that looked almost deliberately drab, because of its lack of texture pattern or colour. It is perhaps the one material where you could say, the reasons why people visually hate it, were exactly the reason why other people loved it.

It is very much a typology material to me. You are unlikely to create very homely and natural-looking architecture with concrete. Whereas museums or public buildings tend to be very commonly made from concrete. It is structurally very strong and so extensively used in high rise towers, floor slabs, and walls. The facing texture effects that can be achieved with concrete are pretty impressive, by applying formwork to create a timber plank type visual, for example. There are a huge number of additives, ingredients, and agents that can be added to the concrete recipe, and worth a few minutes exploring online.

Steel.

Having only been 'invented' for building purposes in the late 1700s in the UK during the industrial revolution, most commonly metal, steel, iron, and aluminium is now somewhat unavoidable in nearly any form of house building. I am not sure it is possible to execute a building project without any metal involved in the final result, let alone, the manufacturing process. There are plenty of variations possible in metal fabrication to achieve extra strength.

A huge proportion of buildings are made from a steel frame, with other materials clad around it as a finish. Even on a small scale, steel comes in channels, beams, sections, and angles, and will certainly be in heavy usage for years to come. It is not a visually pleasing material, bland in colour and no inherent pattern or texture, but because of the span and strength qualities, steel is commonplace in any buildings. I feel like metal and steel is often more of a necessity than a choice for architects.

Glass.

Similarly, to steel, glass has only been around comparatively recently, and typically is seen in cladding applications in high rise and large buildings. Glass is a sustainable building material in theory, and absolutely revolutionary in terms of what it did for human beings and buildings. Perhaps an easy way to describe its application, is to think of the building you live in or the buildings around you now, how would they manage without glass?

For most applications glass is still made using the float

glass process. You will find many online videos, articles, and books showing you all about how glass is made, but very simply it is melted sand mixed with lime and heated, then rapidly cooled. Its usage currently has been around for decades, but has only just been enhanced in terms of the environmental push for improved use since energy reduction and saving became such a central part of our lives. Triple glazed glass units are finally becoming more common, where argon or krypton fill the space between glass panes, which has improved its energy saving benefits.

Glass fundamentally allowed humans to improve their surroundings and their habitat. Natural light in buildings was generally not a concern in domestic design hundreds of years ago. Previously, the installation of glass and windows commonly represented a point of weakness, in terms of heat loss and condensation build-up. Technology, theory, and application has improved to such a level that triple glazing nearly solve these problems. There are several tint and colour variations in the glass 'ingredients,' like extra Sulphur or sodium. There is so much to research here, but I would encourage you to know the basics of float-glass, double-glazing, laminating, and how glass is adapted to resist UV light use in buildings.

Plasterboard.
Plasterboard is another almost essential building product. I can instantly recommend the 'White Book' to you (interestingly called the 'Red Book' in Australia). It is an incredible compendium of internal walls. It's like the book of secrets, in terms of internal walls. Produced using the sulphate mineral called 'gypsum,' it is superbly flexible and usable. The white / red book describes how it all goes together in brilliant detail. I could genuinely pick it up now

and be engrossed for an hour. The way in which it is presented online is also brilliant for learning, so I definitely recommended a read. There are types like moisture resistant, impact resistance, sound-absorbing, and fire rated.

Dislikes.

There are plenty of building styles or materials that I do not like very much in contrast. Generally, I find render finishing and aluminium cladding panels are extremely popular, yet extremely basic and bland in almost all parts of the world. You will be able to see numerous examples nearly anywhere you look. The monochrome cladding panels are so faceless, lacking any personality or enjoyment of generally large parts of a building. And why are they always such a boring mid grey colour? It is very prevalent where I live, here in Melbourne, and it has spoilt certain views of the city. It's painful to see such bland materiality in large facades when just a small effort would drastically improve it. Large buildings with unimaginative patterned facades in huge lines or patterns look horrendous.

There's a couple of phrases I like, such as 'necessity is the mother of invention,' or 'during desperation comes innovation,' or something like that. That's very relevant to building design and materials. Especially in construction techniques, the critical mass point arrives when enough companies or designers have committed to designing something unusual, so eventually the whole industry starts to use it. It is just a trust issue and probably a natural human reaction to be cautious with new products or techniques.

Building a career in architecture

1.5 QUALIFICATIONS POST GRADUATION

1.5.1 First involvement.

1.5.2 Chartered qualification and the interview.

1.5.3 CIAT in the Middle East and Australia.

1.5.4 A second layer of professional qualification.

1.5.1 First involvement

Formed in the 1960s, as an 'institute for the technicians,' CIAT (the Chartered Institute of Architectural Technology) has been a very well recognised UK qualification for many years. The focus is science and technology in architecture, and has provided me with exactly the break away from pure architecture that I wanted. I achieved my CIAT chartership in October 2013, and it has been a focal point of my capabilities ever since. The best way to describe its influence is using the same text from an article I was asked to submit for the CIAT magazine just a few months ago. It was intended to show where my career has taken me, with a brief overview of projects, and how that journey has been largely due to my CIAT qualification and developments from there. So here is that article piece:

"My architectural technologist journey has taken me to 3 countries, with projects located in 6 countries, with 7 architecture and design companies, in the region of about

18-20 projects, located in about 10 different cities. The journey has given me a vast range of experience and exposure to industry reality, which has been most crucial, and that's hugely down to my architectural technology background with CIAT.

I passed the Chartered exam in 2013, about 7 years after graduation, and have been involved in a great array of projects like historic conversions, theme parks, new and repurposed stadiums, mixed-use skyscrapers, high-tech media parks, inventive office fit-outs, and a couple of simple suburban houses. Something I'm really glad about is that my role hasn't actually changed too much since my first job in 2005.

Straight out of university, I wanted to follow the technical design and constructability side of the industry, and initially fitted into the niche of CAD draughtsman, whilst gradually improving my detailing and technical knowledge of all types of building. Now, 19 years after setting off on the architecture degree journey, I still want to be the person who can describe exactly how this building can be put together and what makes good design for the cities and places that we live in. The knowledge I've picked up along the way has allowed me to learn from, and be directly involved with, Clients, Project Managers, Building Authorities, Engineers, Artists, Designers, Builders, and of course, building occupants. I've been able to see the whole design and construction spectrum, which is largely down to my continuing technical development with CIAT.

Of course, there have been many ups and downs along the way, but I can honestly say I've enjoyed my career, and would not be able to muster the motivation for any other industry. I think you really have to value the job that you're getting out of bed to put 9 hours a day into. CIAT has been an extra layer to that interest, and my involvement and friendship with hundreds of members around the globe, during international trips to Dubai, Aarhus, and New Delhi, has added a bulk of support, encouragement, and recognition during my career. CIAT represents the exact part of the industry that I want to be involved in and promote."

A few months into my first job, and therefore, about nine months after graduation, one of my colleagues was talking about a technologists' and technicians' qualification she was working towards, mostly supported by the work she was doing day-to-day in the office. She had followed a similar university course to mine, had about three years of professional experience, and was gradually topping up the different sections of a report, to qualify as an Architectural Technologist. It only took a few minutes of talking to have me interested. I looked at the qualification options and institute website to assess how this could help me. My new position at this company was 'Architectural Assistant,' as were nearly all graduate jobs, but she was looking to have this qualification as an 'Architectural Technologist,' which I soon understood represented a bit more than a graduate position. I realised the qualification would increase my employability and wage, and could be something I could specialise in.

Whilst the education I had been through at university was important, I started to understand that my job came down to the fact that I could quickly and accurately draw something on CAD. Simple as that. I could adhere to the layers, line weights, block conventions, and 'Xref' rules. Plenty of those dry university lectures about heat calculations and ploughing through architectural history books were of no use anymore. In particular, I remember a colleague called James. He didn't really seem bothered about buildings or architecture. He didn't seem bothered about anything apart from payday and supporting his football team. But he was lightning quick at CAD, very heavily relied upon for quick drawings, and was seen as this 'office saviour' for meeting deadlines. I was amazed how important he was, yet how little he seemed to care. To some extent, the person who can produce accurately and quickly will always be in demand. At least at the early career stages, that is what you are there for.

At this stage of my career, it was unlikely I would go back to full-time university. CIAT represented a great way to develop myself in a real environment. At the age of 22, it's tough to have a solid and rigid career plan. My approach was trying to build up my knowledge but also have a good few years in the industry first to see what it has in store. For me it was the advantage of learning more hands on, making important contributions to a real building, and of course, earning money.

1.5.2 Chartered qualification and the interview

With such a huge number of qualifications from all over the world trying to match up, it is difficult to know which universities or accreditations really represent good skills and knowledge. A career is made over years, not months, however much you want to hurry it along, so additional qualifications after university show that attitude for continual improvement.

The more advanced level of CIAT qualification was the Chartered qualification. The assessment was concerning how I had dealt with and understood day-to-day issues in my role. At this point, I did not know much about contracts and high-level client meetings, but the 'knowledge vs understanding' sections made it easy to write down what I have accomplished myself, and then separately what I have just observed or learnt. My submission talked mostly about my Highbury Square facades and windows package, attending consultant and subcontractor meetings and lots of exposure to the cladding, curtain walling and window manufacturers. The supporting evidence I submitted was simple but effective; such as my emails about coordination, marking up a drawing in red pen with a date, creating a basic specification page, conducting site reports, or sending design decisions to the site teams. It was a bit of a crash course in architecture, but it is so much better when you are on a real job and can see some of the things play out in office meetings, overhearing phone calls, or being copied into emails.

I attended the professional interview, at CIAT headquarters in London. I felt relaxed overall, but less so once some questions were being fired at me. The process was centred around explaining my projects and career, my responsibilities and what I had enjoyed about the industry. Although one particular question absolutely shook me up. I was asked about the main amendments to the new UK Part L energy regulations that were released earlier that year. It had me in a sweat. I looked around a bit, to pretend I was going to pluck the answer out of nowhere, but thought I better try to answer with some sort of authority. I had to admit I don't know off-hand about those new regulations. In truth, I had absolutely no idea what the answer was.

Luckily, that answer contributed to my passing of the exam. I referenced my office Technical Department, and the specification writing team leader, saying I would know exactly where to find that information, by taking the advice of these in-house specialists. The CIAT interviewer said it was the honesty that showed I was the right sort of candidate to be approved. That fact that I was not going to take risks and pass the responsibility off, but to be accurate and proactive. Honesty definitely is the best policy!

I was also advised in this interview that there is no harm in asking the same question twice. It is going to potentially save the company a legal case, and save you a very awkward chat with your director about why you did not find out the answer from the department which is set up to do exactly that for you. Sometimes you just need to apologise, ask again, and get on with the job. I felt under pressure from the examiners, but they just wanted to get to know me. In fact, they wanted to pass me, as with everyone else they interview. But they need to rigorously ensure you will represent the institute in the right way.

It was a great relief and pride to get the MCIAT pass. It was a proud moment to have the professional and royal chartered institute behind me, demonstrating my clear position in the industry. It was an improvement on the generic degree that most people had, knowing that my expertise will forever be recognised and I had distinguished myself as a specialist.

1.5.3 CIAT in the Middle East and Australia

My Middle East move in 2014 coincided with the time that CIAT were pushing for international development.

Nobody really took the reins on publicity or communication, so my view of this was a great opportunity to represent the institute, and give me something else aside from work. The benefits were kind of snowballing. Joining the 8 strong Middle East committee had lots of benefits; deciding where to spend the budget, making arrangements or suggestions for events, and potentially attending the council meetings back in the UK. I was exposed to things I would not usually read about, and was learning and developing my own role with people that were senior to me in skills and experience. A hugely important side benefit was knowing who in the committee is working on what project, what role they have, and of course, whether that could lead to job offers and career connections one day.

CIAT has opened my connections to hundreds of people. Globally, it is a good network, so I could easily call upon 20 or 30 people, who would be very willing to say hello and help out in any way they could if I needed them. My involvement has led to attendance at the AGM in London and Aarhus, Denmark, to get a close view of how the institute operates. I led lunchtime seminars about CIAT at my company, encouraging others to develop themselves and undertake the qualification. From the management point of view, if there is a staff member who can develop these schemes independently, that is a huge benefit for them, so they don't have to bother leading it themselves.

1.5.4 A second layer of professional qualification

I think governing your own professional development, outside of the employment sphere gives you a crucial advantage. In my experience it was useful to learn about other companies, people, and techniques being used, and how software was being exploited in ways I had never heard of. Those links and connections can always be helpful for recruitment or job searching. Typically, full time employment does not give much scope for this sort of personal development, so the extracurricular involvement is somewhere you can refine your skills at managing people, organising events, and exposing yourself to other parts of the industry.

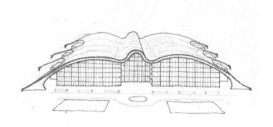

SECTION 2 – CAREER TIPS

2.1 CAREER ADVICE IN 12 STEPS

It is an easy position to be in, dishing out advice based on your own experiences. But in the architecture industry, experience counts for a lot. Especially when trying to secure your first job, any sort of industry experience seems essential. But you will not have experience until you find a job, so this is a difficult 'chicken-and-egg' scenario. Hence earlier references discussing how important it can be to have some work experience or internship during university years or immediately after. Even later in your career, the positions you have held and typologies you have worked on, can be directly influential to your next move or ability to contribute to projects, so that early taster of the industry is such an exciting but crucial step.

This section of the book gives succinct, manageable, and achievable targets, to help shape your career. Some will be helpful to you, some may not, but they are all based on real situations and can otherwise prompt you to develop your own ideas moving forward. Some targets are big, some small, some are easy and some hard. The variety of your experience early on should give a perfect grounding to move into more niche areas or to specialise. Every minute of the day in practice should be valuable to help guide your path forward, but you can start to focus your skills immediately, to lean you towards a certain preference.

I have collated a range of opinions and thoughts from various friends and past colleagues I have met in my career. I asked what their advice would be to their younger self, about getting on in the industry and how to approach it. This hopefully gives you a wide spectrum of interesting opinions and lessons learnt from some great people.

In my early years, I muddled through like everyone else and was not necessarily giving lots of thought to my career path. But having had time to reflect, the below 12 points summarise my best advice for shaping your career and developing a strong resilience to what the world of architectural work will throw at you. I have already discussed some of these topics in more depth in the previous sections, hence partly repeated, but condensed into an easier list here.

As follows:

1. Keep developing software skills.
2. Ask questions.
3. Find a mentor.
4. Confront your weaknesses.
5. Build a vision.
6. Get out there and look around.
7. Keep sketching.
8. Jump into office initiatives.
9. Research the real architecture world.
10. Embrace networking.
11. Consider new qualifications.
12. Shape your architectural identity.

1. Keep developing software skills

Choose a year in the last 50. Any year. You can be sure that the architecture industry wasn't the same 10 years before that, and it was probably quite different 10 years later too. My current career span is still quite brief, but I've seen huge changes, and so will you. My career has been focused on technology and software skills right from the start, but it is good to look back and study the trends in architecture and the changes in the industry.

There are incredible old black and white photos online, showing warehouse sized rooms entirely full of architectural draughtsman, all standing over their huge A0 and A1 drawing boards, dressed nearly identically, with an overhead lamp each, in perfectly arranged rows. Presumably they are working on various packages in this amazing factory style colony, a conveyor belt of drawing production. It is a stunning difference to see how projects were executed and communicated just a few years ago.

Despite being released in the 1980s, AutoCAD developed quickly in the UK and became indispensable by the late 90s. ArchiCAD, SketchUp and other 3D platforms began to develop the visual representation much better, leading to stylish rendering tools giving photographic quality images and lighting effects beyond belief really took over. Soon followed the brilliant integration of Revit and ArchiCAD and all their plug ins, followed by the now fairly common VR, futuristic interpretations of project data, headsets, algorithms, automatically generated designs, and navigating a fully digital building by pointing hand controls. It has been an astonishing change in barely 25 years.

Software defines how we organise and deliver projects. Design teams sit all around the world, collaborating via video calls, contributing to various BIM projects in locations they have never set foot in. This is the current best practice. If you can establish a better way of doing things, you will be a highly sought-after employee. In some ways now, there are so many software packages available, each contributing to many different parts of the project process, so your options are far wider. Previously, employability in early years was almost exclusively centered on CAD ability. Revit and ArchiCAD seem pretty dominant for now, but that's changing too, and you can find your software niche if you keep abreast of current trends.

BIM managers did not really exist 15 years ago. The role has developed because of our reliance on BIM models for the design and construction process. It's fairly non-negotiable that you have to keep learning new software in your career. I'm a big fan of those easily available tutorial videos online, and whilst project experience will always be the best way to learn, the fact that you can bolster those skills or pick up new ones with such minimal effort is a crucial part of future proofing your career.

2. Ask questions

A classic old phrase but completely true in architecture. Everyone is in a junior position at some point in their career, and from what I have seen, it is far better to be interested, talkative and to ask questions, than to be shy, anxious, and quiet. Your early years are really a time to embrace knowledge. Work conversations and relationships need effort, and that comes from a simple act, talking. Talk openly, brightly and give good eye contact, and listen to what people have to say. Be professional, down to earth, intelligent and engage with the whole team. Sounds simple, but when you ask questions of colleagues, make sure the answer sinks in and keep thinking about it that day.

I was not great at this in my first few years. I was a bit anxious to be saying the wrong thing or asking a stupid question. Whether talking aloud on the phone, asking questions of suppliers or trying to contribute to team meetings. In project phone calls, I could not really get the words out smoothly to say who I am and what I am calling about. I was worried how I would sound. There was a couple of times when I decided to go to the toilet to 'calm my nerves' and plan out the call before coming back to my desk to execute it, once I had whispered it to myself privately first. It was just a simple enquiry call to a subcontractor or product supplier, like carpets or bathroom tiles or something. If this sounds like you, some remedies you can try are to practice at home, talking to the mirror, or trying the conversation with family or friends. Introduce yourself clearly, and say what it is you are trying to find out.

For product, manufacturer, or supplier calls, I can suggest to have the website or product page up in front of you on your screen for easy reference if you need it. The person on the other end of the call is probably very helpful and understanding. These relationships can develop over time if you need to speak with them on further occasions. You also build up better knowledge of the products you are calling about.

I would often write down a few questions or uncertainties that may have built up over the course of a few days, secretly hoping that the solution would come along at some point, but if not, asking a question of a colleague. Bottom line is that if you don't know how to do something, you have got to ask. Time is money in any job, so do not sit there stewing in silence for 2 hours, when you could have it solved within 5 minutes of conversation. When you are young and keen, it is ok to ask questions. Colleagues probably expect it. At least colleagues know you will be asking sensible, worthy questions that are helping you learn and getting the task done quicker.

One memorable time I was asked to print a PDF file of my CAD work in my first temporary job. I confidently said yes, I'll do that straight away. Problem was, I didn't actually know how to print a PDF, and sat quite worriedly for about 30minutes, trying to have a guess. My boss had to come over and point out that maybe I didn't know how to print a PDF and he better just show me that it is a 30 second job. I definitely wasted a fair bit of time there, and felt a bit stupid about it.

In the first few weeks of starting a role in London, I unfortunately had to ask about 10 questions a day about learning MicroStation and even worse, it was to a very grumpy and quiet guy so I felt like I was really bugging and interrupting him. But gradually there were less and less questions each day and he realized at least I was improving my skills, which meant less questions. Don't challenge yourself with unknowns. Start questioning and get it done with.

3. Find a mentor

For all those questions you are going to ask above, it might feel like you are causing disruption. Hopefully on the receiving end, is a friendly and patient colleague. Failing that, it is a beneficial short and medium term support if you can find yourself an official mentor. They might not even know they are your mentor at first, but having someone to look up to in their role, attitude and knowledge is very important. They would be ideally someone who's position you would like to be in, 3 to 5 years from now.

Hopefully, your company will have a fairly well organised mentoring scheme. It needs to set good targets, plan out how to achieve them, and then check on progress every few weeks. The whole idea is to have a bit of control over your development, to ensure you are improving.

There was a particular architectural technologist who was in my team in London who became my mentor almost by accident. He didn't even know it for many years. A really nice softly spoken guy, about 15 years older than me, but very technically minded, inquisitive, liked to vent a bit, but really appreciated taking the time to do things properly both for himself and the project. He always found time to talk me through things as well, instead of just throwing out an answer. He liked to sketch things out on his pad although strangely his sketches were quite basic and not always easy to follow. But I was seeing his architectural mind at work. He would happily pick up the phone to get advice too, understanding that he always has something to learn. In this case there was no official mentoring scheme, I just kind of realised after a couple of years I would often turn to him. We had a great working relationship and discussed all other aspects of life too, so he was a kind of default mentor.

It is a crucial step for your own development to reach out and say you would like some guidance over a few months and years, and then to form a strong, trusting friendship with someone. It's a tough career pushing through the first five years or so, and even harder when you develop a few more responsibilities and take a more prominent role. Simple mentoring conversations that helped me, were; how to behave in meetings, how my role overlaps with others, how are different companies paid, and then who pays for delays in construction.

Share targets with your mentor and establish checkpoints, e.g., in the next month I'd like to have three conversations with you about building contracts and project stages. Or by the end of the year, I want to know about five floor details, five roofing systems, and five external wall types. It's all about absorbing knowledge and plugging little holes that you know are there.

I enjoy mentoring to pass on the knowledge I have, but it often throws up areas I need to improve too, so it works both ways. I currently mentor anything from 3-6 people with varying frequency of contact.

There were a million things I wanted to know in my early and mid 20s in architecture, and it took a while to answer them, but I really pushed myself to talk to people in the office if I liked the way they did something. That first little chat would turn into a few more coffee machine chats, then quite a close working relationship builds up. Soon you will be encouraged by some moral support, knowing someone is looking out for you.

4. Confront your weaknesses

Similarly to mentoring, if there is something you are not so good at, and you need to improve it, it will not get better if you sit there and picture how bad it's going to get. There is plenty of help around you when you need it, and for sure there has been no better time in history to have a quick question so easily answered, through the endless supply of websites and knowledge building resources. Your mentor can obviously help here, but it needs that self-drive to attack it first. It is easy to be a bit scared by things you don't know, or to feel out of your depth, but you must confront that. A big step is to identify issues and realise they need improvement.

I had an obvious weakness in my first few years. I was a bit afraid of the basic construction knowledge that I thought I should have. There is too much to learn instantly, but at that point I hardly even knew how a simple domestic house went together. Perhaps it was leftover bruising from my university experience of horrendous crits and soul-destroying presentations. It was a really stinging feeling. Construction detailing and building methodology was not covered in anywhere near the depth I thought it would or should be. It left a big hole of knowledge. I hadn't ever ignored advice or given up learning new things, but the knowledge just wasn't there yet. Suddenly a raft of acronyms, trade names, building terms and industry phrases were thrown about in the office. I had to concentrate to hear the terms, quickly think or guess what it is all about, and by that time the conversation had gone on and totally lost me.

I looked up so many architectural terms in my first few years. Literally thousands. Simple architectural descriptions, like glass types, concrete finishes, door fixings or installation techniques, what grout is, what is a ceiling void for, nearly anything. Don't go another day or another week not knowing what something is. Over several months and eventually years (in fact I am still doing it now) I push to know how something works, what it is made of, or how it is crucial to construction. You can do the same.

5. Build a vision

Short, medium and long-term targets won't be set in stone, and often won't fully work out, but knowing approximately what you are trying to achieve each month or year, will help develop a strong career path. It could be software improvement, could be working on a skyscraper, could be working for one or two particular architects you admire, it could be travelling to experience a particular building up close. Just note down some short, medium and long-term targets. Even if you only achieve a few of them that's still progress.

After a couple of years in practice, my target soon became getting chartered for CIAT. That became my short to medium term goal. Additionally, I kept a notebook of quick terms to research further, which was a short-term plan. It was mostly construction terminology, but often a building I had seen in literature or on a website, or learning about historical styles of architecture.

A mid-term goal was to attend more client and design team meetings and get some site experience. Everyone else in the office seemed to go off on days out at meetings or site visits, which I wasn't really exposed to. After a few months in my first role, I casually mentioned to the façade package leader, whether I could attend a few meetings to listen in and learn. I was too nervous to make any contribution to the meeting of course, but to sit there and observe a serious professional meeting was great. Even better when there was a bit of a disagreement going on or some real problems to discuss. Your project architect or director should be looking out for you and helping your development.

A more recent and simpler short-term example was having moved to Australia, to learn the regulation AS 1428. This is very similar to what Part M for accessibility covers the UK, so my knowledge was broadly in the right area already, but I did not want to get caught out on it, so it was few months of getting well acquainted with that. A long-term target still in the very distant future is to design and build my own house, which seems at least a decade away, but it is worth having something big to keep working towards.

6. Get out and travel

A very simple piece of advice is, get out there and look at buildings. A lot of my education (which gradually turns into great knowledge and understanding) was to take a proper interest in buildings around me. I was spoilt by living in an architectural and historical city like London for seven years, so hopefully where you live it should not be too hard to get out and start analysing architecture. Even if you are analysing ugly architecture, that is still learning. If it's cold and rainy outside, tough luck, get out there and look at the world around you. Take it all in and feed your mind with the architectural wonders or total disasters. Whatever amazing images you find of a building online, they most likely show a limited angle of the building in real life. Seeing the building set in its real context is extremely valuable.

A very frequent lunchtime challenge I committed to whilst in London, was to get straight out of the door for my one hour lunch break, and set off on a brisk walk, maybe 20 mins in one direction, just to take it all in. Visually studying buildings and their setting, cramming in some lunch whilst walking. When you are in full time work, that lunch hour becomes really valuable. Companies often do lunchtime sketching clubs which is a great idea, although you can still do this alone. Even better, start an office lunchtime club and set up historical walking routes or interesting buildings near your office. There will be so many interesting little examples of design just minutes or seconds away from where you live or work, but you will not learn from them unless you just go and take a look.

During the Construction in Architecture module at university, part of the submission requirement was to visit a building site, take photos, and provide a written report of what was being built and what techniques were being used. It was a live building site of pretty standard semi-detached housing in my hometown. Despite being a bit embarrassed to ask, I drove up to the site office, asked for the site Foreman, and requested a quick ten minute tour for the purposes of my university education. I took about 30 photos of various foundations being dug out, damp proof coursing, external walls, internal partition frames going up, and some structural openings of doors ready to be completed. It was amazing seeing the site workers holding muddy, crumpled architects' drawings in their hands and constructing exactly what someone like me might have been drawing on CAD the previous day.

I would hugely encourage doing this if you want to improve your construction knowledge. You might unfortunately get a negative response if the site is too busy, or be asked to come back some other time, but if you can even just walk past local construction sites and peer through the site boundary, or take a few minutes to observe what is happening, or maybe even track progress over a few months, it's probably the best sort of learning you can get.

On the wider scale of experiences, travel and cultural understanding has been vital. I have ended up in the variety of locations in my career directly because of a passion for travelling and learning about other parts of the world. It is really exciting to see globally famous cities and understand the basics of a place first of all. Learning about the history and development, then finding hidden gems, private houses or small boutique projects that would only be shown in specific architectural textbooks is great.

I am always trying to understand how and why each building was designed, made or changed. Most cities have a strangely reliable pattern of development; a large, impressive place or worship, then a highly decorated classical town square or plaza, a historical quarter or district, then a modern slick shopping center, maybe a structurally beautiful train station, then probably hundreds of nice little tight city buildings, housing pubs, residences, shops and museums. Be inquisitive and keep finding architecture interesting. If by chance you find places boring and lifeless, then at least analyse them and know why you find them to be a turn off. Critically appraise everything around you, like you are a scholar of global architecture. And take a hell of a lot of photos.

7. Keep sketching

This won't be easy to maintain, but whenever a chance presents itself either at work or home, quickly take opportunities to sketch something. Perspective, plan views, a concept, or more serious still-life drawing can be beneficial and relaxing. Have some spare scrap paper around and pens nearby, and feel the freedom and enjoyment of a quick drawing. I always found it especially good to understand construction detailing by sketching things out whether at home or in the office.

Remember that some of the most celebrated and famous architectural icons of the world have come from a very simple first sketch. By drawing only four or five lines in a sketch, you can often know what the building is. Think of the Eiffel Tower, the Burj Khalifa, the Pentagon, Sydney Opera House, the Shard in London, the Empire State building, even the Pyramids or Stonehenge. They could all be represented easily in about five seconds of drawing. Having that quick catchy way of representing something visually is a great skill. It's not always the aim of producing a nice sketch, but the hand to eye coordination and training yourself is crucial to improving.

My trouble with sketching was always scale and proportion. I could never quite get the sizing of sketches quite right, and drawing the human face was always a nightmare. At a later stage in your career, it can be argued you won't need sketching skills and of course with great software skills is might not become important. But it is a reminder that you are still in an artistic subject. Architecture is inherently artistic. If it were not, every building, home, office or station would just be an identical square box.

8. Jump into office initiatives

A happy workforce is likely to be a productive and therefore successful workforce. Pretty simple stuff, but staff initiatives are a brilliant way to develop your early career, show yourself as a keen and enthusiastic member of the team, and even practice some team leader skills. After many years of being involved in these, I can say they were hugely valuable to my development, and great for social life as well.

Leading these activities and being involved is not exactly going to secure you promotion, but at the same time it's a way to show that you are proactive, can organise, and can play a team role. Get involved with external and extra-curricular activities in the office, and if there isn't any, start them up. Social clubs, sports, yoga, local architecture walks, life drawing, I have seen them all in offices, and started quite a few. Not only for your own expression and enjoyment, but for mental health and social development. Architecture offices make a big deal of these extra activities, so there's good lessons to be learnt from organizing and directing people more senior than you.

One memory that sticks out for me is the green office week. It was a great initiative in the UK whereby various businesses, mostly in architecture, pushed to highlight and engage in greener practices. I took a leading role in this and one task was to go around the office (120 people or so) and request they empty their side drawers of all the unused pens, pencils and stationery they no longer needed. The intention was to show how much wasted company property we had sitting there. Kind of embarrassing looking back, and occasionally people looked a bit threatened as I approached their area of the office, but this recovered a few hundred items back into circulation from years hidden dormant in drawers. Most people in the office found it all quite funny and it stimulates a bit of conversation about the wider message being conveyed. These things were all about trying to be progressive, trying to make positive change, but with the social team attitude closely following.

The company CAD group was also a highlight, by making a fun cartoon-filled presentation featuring ways to improve the CAD protocols and standards. This was actually a massive benefit to the company, raising crucial understanding of controlling project files and reducing the massive cost of data storage. Server speeds and back-up archiving was running into tens of thousands of pounds, but just from jumping in and thinking about some office initiatives to encourage better practice, it made a significant difference to my recognition in the company, with a bit of leadership and comedy thrown in.

You may have a pretty plain CV at 22 years old which is to be expected. However, you will probably need a few extra things there after a few years in practice. If by 30 years old you have only worked at one company on very similar projects, with no extra initiatives, no clubs or teams, no charitable activities, then you are slightly less employable than someone who gets involved, looks for the new fresh ideas and is willing to put a few extra hours in.

9.   Research the real architecture world

The internet has to be the most mind blowing and life changing invention in history. You cannot comprehend life before it now that you have lived with it a few years. And so, on that note, use it for all it's worth. Use it to your massive advantage. You can research anything at almost any time, for the most obscure item or bizarre architectural building. It is difficult to get your head around the breadth of what you can research or find. What worked for me a few years ago was to have a few go-to architectural, design and construction websites as my favourites, to have a quick browse through every day.

Examples being: dezeen.com, detail.com, architectureanddesign.com, constructionweekly.com, buildingdesign.co.uk, there are many more. When you are not sure what something is, and can't ask a question about it to your colleague, research it. Thousands of times I have quickly looked something up in a flash to save myself in a conversation.

Years ago, I was told an interesting part of short-term memory capability. If you learn something now, then relearn it again in the next 30 seconds, learn it again in the next hour, then again the next day, it will stick in your long-term memory. That's an astonishing way to exploit the power of the mind. Even if only 50 / 60% of them sink in, you will know a hell of a lot more in six months than you do now. Try to expand your architectural vocabulary every day, and check in with what's being built and designed around the world or in your city. World news can be pretty depressing at times, so stick to the architectural version.

10. Embrace networking

Something I didn't really take to initially in my early years was that buzzword of 'networking'. I thought I was social enough to not need this extra level of professional socializing. But the point is to get involved with the wider architecture community. Go to talks, exhibitions, listen to podcasts, use LinkedIn, seminars and evening presentations. Either by yourself or with colleagues, be open to finding out where someone else works and what they do.

Starting a conversation with a stranger is a difficult skill, but within the architectural circles you have something in common to begin with. There is always something to learn just from hearing other people's opinions. Attend supplier lunchtime presentations whenever possible (they often provide lunch!) or exhibition events at museums. Lots of this content is readily available online as well, like the

Architecture Social run by an old colleague of mine.

You will find most people in the industry are friendly and will enjoy a quick chat. It may come in very handy when you are looking for a new role, need a favour or an introduction, or want to learn about other companies. Especially when talking to suppliers and subcontractors, being in the architectural circle is a valuable position because they will want you to choose their products for your current project.

11. Consider new qualifications

Generally, you should be aware how the industry is moving and what new trends are taking place. In my early years, the trend was towards green architecture, sustainability, and energy production from buildings, hence plenty of colleagues achieved BREEAM certification in London, then LEED certification in America or the Middle East. People in Europe started looking closely at the 'Passivhaus' movement too.

After my graduation, it was the CIAT qualification was important for me, then attaining some basic Revit skills, then completing the LEED assessment. A qualification should of course align with where you want to be in a few years' time. For example, any successful company in the current climate usually has a BIM manager or digital delivery leader, which was never really required as a job titled a couple of decades ago. In ten years from now, the roles will have further developed, so knowing what's necessary for companies to thrive is interesting. Companies spend a lot of time looking for the next technology opportunities and future design trends, so that the company is making the most efficient use of their software.

Typically, I have found only around 50-60% of the software capacity is actually used to produce drawings for a project. Using Revit or ArchiCAD to its fullest potential is often not needed. But companies must innovate, often reluctantly. No company can be the same now when compared to ten years ago.

When I was between jobs in the past year, I took some time to learn new modelling skills with the software's built-in tutorials, then also completed a course through HarvardX online, called The Architectural Imagination. Whilst not hugely challenging, and I don't get a career defining achievement out of it, it was an interesting topic to study, keeps my learning ticking over, and adds another little feature to my career.

Ensure you are regularly looking for the new industry directions that might need training, qualifications, or expertise in a few years. The trick is to know effort vs benefit. Will a small amount of effort give a big reward? Can companies adopt easy software for big results? From your personal point of view, are you looking at a major qualification that will still be relevant ten years later, or just something to secure you a short-term role? You can really get ahead of the game in this sense, but you have to know what the market wants.

12. Shape your professional Identity

Early in your career, and potentially changeable later on, you can start to establish your preferences and specialism in the industry. By that, I mean your area of expertise in certain typologies, preference of design style, or even style of drawing. You might want to be a jack of all trades in the industry and be able to adjust to any project, but after a few years work it can be good to say you are really into hotel projects, or stadiums, or heritage preservation buildings. Maybe you're solely into digital design or virtual reality.

From typology point of view, do you prefer modernist or classic architecture? What do you think of the robotic, machine orientated 'high-tech' architectural age (influenced by Richard Rogers for example), and is it still popular? Take time to find out what are the historical, social and political beginnings of architectural styles, and why they developed the way they did.

I was a standard CAD monkey for several years, then was drawn by the more technical side of architecture. I was never really on the journey to being a project runner, so my roles were the management of design team consultants, being the point of call for the whole project team, and giving technical advice on products or buildability. I had some site experience which could have restricted me as a delivery architect or package leader. I preferred the construction side compared to early-stage concepts. I personally like to have a noticeboard or pin board space where current designs can be discussed. Currently I'm in the world of specifications, which is an area that many architecture professionals hardly ever touch, so you never know which area of the industry you might find yourself in.

Overall advice – positivity and progression

So, from those items above, if you have got all of them ticked off, you are doing pretty well. Some of them are ongoing and will never stop, but some will get outdated and will change. They will come and go at different stages which is completely understandable. Be positive and remain inquisitive.

2.2 PEOPLE AND PERSONALITIES

The best and worst of my past colleagues

In your career you will experience the weird, wonderful and bizarre variety of people who contribute to the architectural industry. It still makes me laugh looking back at the mix that I have met. Any company success is down to its people and their teamwork. Observing and understanding those combinations will benefit your progression, and probably provide some amusement too. It will become natural to compare yourself with others, but employees at a similar level to you will become invaluable. I am a true believer that effective learning comes from both good and the bad experiences, and there will be plenty of good and bad people you will meet.

Surrounding yourself with star performers could be quite daunting, and their skillsets might dwarf yours. Conversely if you are the stand out employee in your office, you might not have anyone to look up to. You can have all the knowledge in the world, with degrees, qualifications, drawings skills, software skills, and team management theory, but unless you have spent a few years in the industry seeing what really counts, all that knowledge falls flat. It all contributes to your ability to deal with the most problematic part of building projects, which is people.

I have worked with some great people over the years. Firstly, the really sharp designers who can sketch and discuss a simple but compelling idea, often capturing your imagination within a minute or two. Secondly the very well-organized project runners and directors have really gained my respect from their project execution skills, knowing exactly what has to happen and when, understanding and dealing with the background politics, and making level headed decisions despite everyone else perhaps losing their cool. Bottom line is you will not have projects to work on, unless people in your company are driving projects to completion, keeping clients happy, and then bringing in the next project. I have never had to do that myself but I bet it is tough. Thirdly, I listened to the technically minded staff in my early career and that's what I ended up specialising in. To know exactly what companies are out there producing building products on a consistent basis is really handy to the design team, but also being able to instantly analyse the detail and construction is very valuable.

A final type of colleague I gravitate towards is simply someone who talks enthusiastically about architecture. Those who can identify hundreds of amazing buildings from around the world in an instant, know the architect, key features and finer details. People who are visibly excited by architectural chat every day, whether they are discussing an old project, a success or failure, or just a building and company they really admire. That's really infectious to me, and makes you realise how big the subject is.

Contrary to the above positives, I have worked with some really odd, difficult and just not particularly bright people as well. Each of them contributes in their own way to the daily architecture practice. I wondered how on earth they had come to work in the industry, and even more how they have hung on so long. Bad news is, that you will probably work directly with them at some point too. A big part of executing architectural projects is down to how the people combine and work together. Fall outs and disagreements will happen, but as with day-to-day disagreements in any part of your life, the level headed and thoughtful person usually comes out best. Certainly a 'think before you speak' lesson. Architecture is a very subjective industry, so working with people, and compromising, is a big part of it.

If professional relationships ever become strained and potentially damaging, it is good to keep in touch with your project director about it, and speak face to face to resolve things. Otherwise, an email explanation, so that you are not accidentally going to say something in the heat of the moment. Everyone comes home at the end of the day and complains about work, colleagues, or company policies, so welcome to the club, work is not always fun. For the people you don't immediately hit it off with, you might need to understand what makes this person tick. Do they want to chat with you? Maybe they prefer their colleagues to do their job and shut up? Be aware some architectural staff can be pretty stiff and grumpy. You will need to try to spot their style, and work with it. Everyone has probably had a difficult boss or manager at some point, but getting good personal communication with your immediate project team is vitally important to establishing trust and transparency. The first few years in industry will be pretty hard work, so expect a few late nights, personality clashes, tough deadlines and plenty of abortive work.

Relationships work two ways, so analyse yourself

Conversely, how you act in the office works the other way too. Be very aware that people will be observing you and seeing how you handle yourself. Here is where my advice is generally, be quite normal. If your personality is a bit extroverted, it will soon shine through. But for certain times in early career years or starting a new job, you'll need to be professional and keep it simple. Similarly with your approach to other staff, you would want them to give you a chance, learn about you, understand you, and crucially try to help you as a co-worker striving for the same goal. Appreciating the variety of skills in your immediate team should give you a good lesson as to the teamwork involved. Nobody can do all of the jobs, so everyone's skills contribute at different times.

Some colleagues will have built a reliable and trusted reputation within the company, purely by being very reasonable, level headed, careful, or introverted. I can remember a few staff members like this, who I took several months to get to know very well because they did not say too much early on. They were absolutely consistent every day, producing good work, being a good person, maybe quiet, but providing a very stable attitude to the workload. Each style has its importance among a varied team of skills and personalities. Some colleagues might not necessarily be the most exciting, entertaining characters, but definitely the sort of person I want in my team when project deadlines are looming.

A team of skills

Put yourself in managerial shoes for a moment; part of that job is to stand back, observe how your team operates together. Who gets on with who? Who takes control? Who is slightly picky? Is there a maverick in the team? Who shouts first and thinks later? Who takes time to think and speaks later? Then most importantly, who in the team actually has the fundamental skills you need to complete the project deliverables? Which of all those characteristics above is most important? You will probably fit into one of those descriptions in the eyes of your manager, dependent on your behaviour.

I can definitely remember times when I have had to slightly alter my behavior based on colleagues or situations. You can joke a lot with some people but far less with others. Each employee has been hired for a reason, so you can start to understand the company as a whole, and what it needs in order to keep operating. You would not want 90% of people in the office to be identical. Projects need visual skills, technical skills, organizational skills, client relationship skills, construction knowledge, sometimes conflict resolutions skills, amongst many others. They all fit together to make a team.

2.3   PAST COLLEAGUES ADVICE IN 150 WORDS

I wanted to include a quick snapshot of architecture professional's advice, in addition to mine. Below are some short passages of advice from a variety of colleagues I have met over the years. I asked them for their thoughts, in around 150 words, on progressing in the architecture industry and what advice they would give to their 22-year-old self, looking back on their career. This is a good sample of great people who I have got on well with over the years, who were happy to contribute to this book and to your understanding of the early years.

181

Alan – early 40s, Technology and Design Regional leader. I worked directly with Alan in the Middle East for nearly 5 years.

Embrace your time at university. You have an opportunity to be completely free with your design ideas, unhindered by commercial drivers in the "real world". You will learn how to work within these constraints when you start practicing. In the meantime, let loose and have fun.

Also, take every opportunity to work collaboratively with your peers & tutors. Sure, there will be plenty of times where you need to focus and work alone, but constant communication of ideas with your peers at university will help build the communication skills needed for working collaboratively with other architects and consultants on live projects.

Alison – early 30s, Architect. I worked on separate projects in the same architecture office as Alison for 5 years in London.

Architecture is not one-role-fits-all, it is a myriad of responsibilities, technical, creative, visual, artistic, speech skills. University gives you the opportunity to find what you like, or do not like and to determine what sort of career you want to pursue. So, if you do not enjoy elements of your course do not fear – you can find a role in the real world that suits. In this ilk, my advice for any architectural student is to embrace everything. Read a variety of architectural theory, travel (even just within the city you live) and notice the differences. Never be afraid to question; why that material, why that position, what is it creating, does it fulfil its purpose – there is never a wrong question or viewpoint, and only greater knowledge to be gained. By noticing what questions can be asked, you can also prepare your answers for your own crits; or have references to compare and raise commentary on. Be individual, stand by your views, be accepting of other criticism – it is not personal, but merely a form to distinguish your projects strengths and true agenda.

Steve – early 30s. Architecture recruitment. I worked in the same architecture office as Steve for 5 years in London.

Architects come from all walks of life and have overcome obstacles along the way. It is a very hard journey along the path of Architecture. I have been there as a student, 3am with no sleep and the printer is jammed. Stressful? Yes! Memories of trying to enter the job market as a Part I with no experience during recession. Worrying? Definitely. The thrill of your first job in industry? Amazing! Working in architecture has its ups and downs. We all love the industry for different reasons, however whether it is external events or problems within practice sometimes it can feel like the odds are against you and leave you feeling anxious.

Sometimes we all need a little help or would like the support of someone else who is familiar with the industry, even if it is just someone to talk to. Remember that community is important, and your friends, colleagues and especially family can help you through tricky times. If you haven't found a community yet, especially in an online world that we are in - go out there and look. That has been the best bit of the Architecture Social, the community. You don't need to go it alone!

Joanne — early 40s. Architect. I worked directly alongside Joanne in an architecture office for 5 years in the Middle East.

Success is defined by only one person - YOU! It is defined by the goals and victories you set for yourself. Success can be defined in many ways. If you are experiencing happiness, love or adventure in this moment, you've already found success. Do not let fear overpower you but instead work hard to overcome your fears. Remember that losing a few battles will help you win the war and achieve success. Live on and persevere Faith, whether it is from a higher being or the strength of one's character, is the one thing that successful people would say got them through tough times. Believing that everything will turn out for the better when all else fails develops strong character. Success is achieved by overcoming hurdles and persevering over trials encountered. Planning for the unexpected would seem ridiculous at this point. The key is to be flexible and adaptable to any situation and always think towards reaching your goal. Leverage the skills and resources you developed through the years. This could be in the Success is defined by only one person - YOU! September 20, 20203 form of talent or even money saved in the bank. Use these resources to start your passion project, you never know where this will take you. We hear many stories of people who after losing their jobs, started a food business and ended up earning much more than their nine to five jobs. If you ask them about it, they say the feeling of fulfillment are upon them at this point.

Claire – early 40s. Heritage architect. I worked under Claire for 7 years in a practice in London.

My guiding principle for my career has been to be open minded about the breadth of the construction industry: there is so much to learn from others who work alongside in parallel specialisms. Site experience, particularly, has been a rich place for learning how disciplines work together to contribute to the built environment. Learning how to communicate effectively with a huge range of people is fundamental to achieving a positive outcome and builds meaningful leadership skills. The construction industry is about people, and networking in a fashion that you are comfortable with is a powerful means to propel your career and broaden your scope. As your horizon is widened you need to be clear on your career aims to enable you to make appropriate decisions. Finding a mentor you can confide with can have a huge impact in navigating your career journey. From experience I recommend looking for a mentor who is outside your immediate profession to benefit from an objective perspective. Most of all don't be afraid to try things out! Everyone has a unique set of experiences which combine to make each of our journeys our own.

Fabio – mid 40s. Architect and Regional Practice Technology Leader. I worked in the same architecture office as Fabio for 2 years in London.

It is well known that information is KING but managing

information and knowledge is POWER! The AECO industry (Architecture, Engineering, Construction and Owner-operated industry) is becoming more and more data-centric which means that business will take decisions based on data so skills to analyse and process data will become very important. Programming skills is a fundamental quality for future professionals in the AECO industry, and you will be able to develop applications to resolve complex design solution. Structured Data is a crucial factor to promote a revolution in our industry. The process to interact with your colleagues is imperative to your success, so developing soft skills (social skills) for communication, character, or personality will support your career.

Andy – late 40s. Architectural technologist. I worked directly with Andy in the same architecture office for 7 years in London.

'All that I know is that I know nothing...' words of a wise man. Leaving college and starting out in architecture and construction you may think you have all the answers, gleaned from terms of hard study, but until you have put building block upon building block upon building block, there is much still to learn. You can know what you want to achieve from design and you must protect it from unscrupulous souls who look for an easy life, but at the same time there are many ways to achieve perfection, using the knowledge of others who have layered those building blocks before. It is down to you to choose and control which path to take, which compromise will have little or no effect on the overall outcome and which trade-off keeps all parties happy on the walk along the

construction path.

Julian — mid 30s. Graduate Architect. I worked with Julian in Australia.

Don't be seduced by the glossy architectural renders and fancy websites of the offices you would like to work for. Large practices tend to silo workers into smaller teams — which means you will get stuck doing bathroom elevations and other construction documentation packages. Offices tend to bring on graduates for certain stages of projects and then terminate once that project is completed, try to reach out to someone who has worked for the office you intend on applying for to find out how often they cycle through employees or if they are more likely to invest.

Smaller offices that specialise in single dwelling residential / smaller scale typologies will often invest more time in your development, you will probably get more exposure to all stages of the design process and you will be able to more freely express and contribute your ideas to the projects.

Some architectural offices have quite negative cultures, encouraging long hours and a very hierarchical structure — on face value they are hard to identify but I would suggest doing some research before signing on. In an interview remember they are selling you the role as much as you are trying to sell yourself. Don't just take a job for the sake of getting in, be patient and find the right organisation for you.

Shantelle — early 20s. Architecture student. I was

mentoring Shantelle for 3 years in her early career through university studies

I chose to do an architectural technology with foundation course at university and was so excited to learn, graduate, get a job and live doing my passion for the rest of my days. Things were very far from that simple list. I would let it be known to anyone just starting out to imagine the path of an architect or AT as a squiggly line all over the place, rather than a straight line (with many fun, new things to learn on the way). Truth be told, my passion slowly started decreasing over the years because of fear of not being good enough. What played a part in this fear was my youthfulness and not understanding it could be my greatest advantage in the field, however I saw it as a great setback. I kept fueling my fears by telling myself I'm so young and lack knowledge and experience.

During my last year I was lucky enough to work on a real-life project which put some fight back in me and not only did I find that yes, I was gaining the experience that I wanted and needed but I also was using skills and knowledge that I had already had in me from over the years...so the person who was judging my competence the most was myself!

My drive began to pick back up when I realised I was able to spot my own weaknesses and better them and grow outside of the classroom as well as inside. But I have learnt a very important lesson; you cannot get ahead of the race and don't try to. Everyday there will always be something you don't know.

I am very content with where I am now and loving it. Some tips I would recommend to develop confidence are: reading a lot from construction books, AT magazine, etc., watching videos, getting a mentor, and surrounding yourself around people of similar interests. You can't go wrong!

Yves — late 30s. Architect. I worked in the same architecture office as Yves for 7 years in London.

Architecture is a big commitment. This can induce worry and stress at any point during one's career. However, I wanted to use my contribution to this project to outline an optimistic view. The world of construction is so vast, to this day, I still encounter new disciplines and experts that I would never have expected were involved in building buildings. Maybe this is due to change in legislation or change in technology perhaps, but it does mean there is always a bewildering array of options available to you should you change your mind or perhaps want to try something new. Everything you learn and experience along the way is valuable, I would say, go with the flow, see what excites you along the way. It's very useful to make a note of what you like and what you don't. You may find this is difficult to do to begin with, but this can become clearer when comparing with other experiences. This can really help make choosing what to do for your next step much simpler (which might be to stay where you are - but even this decision is made easier by going through a careful thought process). The basic point I'm getting at is, there is no need to worry about making the wrong decision, if something doesn't work out, you can change it. From historic buildings to fire safety to integrated home cinema specialists, there are options and opportunities all with transferable skills. Enjoy buildings, enjoy life, have fun discovering where it takes you!

James — late 30s. Architect. I worked in the same London practice as James for 7 years in London.

The important thing to remember when engaged in the process of design is the respective talents of the team around you; that can be in your company, or as part of a project. Some people are organised - I suggest you let them get on with it. Some people aren't - don't hold it against them, they have other (very useful) qualities, such as improvisational thinking and a solid bullshit generation engine... and maybe a good bullshit radar too. When dealing with arseholes, respect the situation: you will never be able to be more of an arsehole to them, than they are to you - you merely have the motivation, they have that as well as both talent and inclination on their side... and they've been at it longer than you have. So, remember through all this that the person more disorganised than you is letting you get on with it, the person who is more organised than you are relying on you to sniff out the bullshit and run interference, and nothing you will ever do will upset an arsehole more than leaving them to their own devices. Don't forget that at any given point you are one or all of these people, and don't be afraid to forgive yourself accordingly - find joy where you can, and always seek ways to find more of it.

Sahar — late 30s. Architect. I worked in the same practice as Sahar for 5 years in Middle East.

If I was to give a 20-odd year-old graduate of

architecture some career advice, I would tell them to establish a long-term goal on where they want to be in their career in 20+ years. Then set a strategy for how to get there, in 5-year increments, and be flexible with that strategy; reassess it every few years to be sure it is still relevant to the long-term goal, as well as the person they grow to become as they move forward in life. Pay careful attention to the importance of hobbies and extra curriculum activities that you choose in life and how they will influence your career strategy. Finally, keep (even a distant) association with educational institutions.

Chris — mid 30s. BIM manager. I worked in the same architecture office as Chris for 5 years in London.

Specialise! Architecture is an incredibly broad profession of boundless knowledge, and no single architect can possibly know everything about every building type, function, material, process, product or style, and be gifted creative designer on top of all that.

As an architect in practice, it's easy to fall into the trap trying to know a little about everything, a jack of all trades. You become a half decent designer, who can make visualisations, 3d models, draft their own drawings, but when it comes to anything tricky you lean on the knowledge and experience of others. Being an all-rounder makes you an incredibly useful resource, but sadly so are most of your peers. It's quite easy to become just another number in the pool of production staff doing the legwork for others. Depending on where you work, time and efforts are generally not well acknowledged or rewarded, and it can be difficult to move forward in your career.

The culture in many studios often implies that design skills are valued above all else. In reality good building design also requires equal amounts of mathematics, engineering, and science. If being creative doesn't come naturally to you, gracefully accept it. There are many equally important contributions to be made.

My advice to any architect who has nailed down the basics is to specialise. Find the aspect of architecture you particularly enjoy, such as sustainability, heritage, digital technology, visualisation, computational design, construction detailing, specification, project management or even a particular type of building such as hospitality, rail or health care. Become the expert if your studio of what you enjoy, research, do courses and build up valuable knowledge. Having expert knowledge can allow you to progress into new roles, stand out as a leader in your practice, educate others and make valuable contributions to projects doing something you enjoy.

Greg — mid 30s. Architect. I worked in the same architecture office as Greg for 2 years in the Middle East

Each of us has unique talents, skills, passions, and values - never lose sight of your own. You will find more enjoyment and success in your career if it aligns with what you are passionate about. So how do you start? Find a firm that shares your philosophy towards design and focuses on projects that excite you. Seek out mentors, inside and outside the firm, that are in a position where you'd like to be; whether that's 5 years from now or 30 years from now. Ask questions, soak up experience, and never stop growing your talents and challenging your what matters to you. And what if your position doesn't find you in the right firm or surrounded by the right people? There is value in every experience. Always try to find this value and use it to move toward your passions and goals.

Jamie – late 20s. Architectural technologist. I met Jamie through CIAT trips and institute involvement.

Entering the architectural profession and construction industry will provide a you a role that changes daily and is a continual learning curve from the day you start university right through your career. Not only do products develop, the way we design continues to change and the regulations we work to react to ensure our buildings are fit for purpose and ultimately keep users safe.

Design software has particularly been an element within my own career that I have worked on from using AutoCAD to now delivery multi-million-pound projects using Revit with an international design team – this being a particular achievement to date.

I have always worked closely with my aligned professional body – 'The Chartered Institute of Architectural Technologists' CIAT. This have provided incredible opportunities, not just a vast network of industry professionals but the opportunity to travel, from India to Denmark. Being involved allows me to understand the importance of such an institute and important matters that effect our industry.

The one driving factor being my shear enjoyment of my role is working away for months on a detailed pack of drawings and then walking around the construction site seeing skilled construction workers bringing the drawings to life – for me this is a great feeling and keeps me invested each day in my work.

I always used to look around me at the land, buildings, infrastructure and considered how on earth these things all worked, who designed what or how these actually stood up. I was always technically minded at school and really enjoyed the drawing and designing elements of certain school classes. If anyone has these similar thoughts my advice would be to get involved, by this it doesn't strictly mean attend university immediately, site experience is considerably valuable, apprenticeship schemes provide a great insight to the industry and where possible throughout school years push for work experience in design practices, with contractors or on site. All of the above will assist in making a well-rounded construction professional. Also, never be scared to ask a question – you will always continue to learn if you ask.

And one from me – Joseph, late 30s. Chartered Architectural Technologist, working in Specifications.

You won't know where you'll be in 5 years' time, and you've probably changed a lot from 5 years ago, so appreciate that the architectural world is changing all the time. That means there are so many opportunities in exactly the right role for you, so establishing short medium and long term goals should help. Hopefully this career is going to last about 40 years, so you have plenty of twists and turns ahead of you, and lots of time to do different things.

Relevant skills are really important, arguably more important than your education, so keep up with the most common software and ensure you can operate it really competently. Architecture is still an art form, but lots of day-to-day life is simply sitting on a computer, modelling and making up sheets and details. Research and learning should be ongoing, but don't be too exasperated by the sheer amount of knowledge about the subject. You just have to know your level and know what you can offer at that time.

I think it's important to divide your architecture employment against your enjoyment and interest in architecture as a hobby. You definitely need to be happy at work, so try to find what is going to keep you enthusiastic about your work, because that will resonate through your life too.

2.4 TALKING ARCHITECTURE

2.4.1 Reading about and describing architecture

2.4.2 Describing architecture to a novice

2.4.3 My favourite buildings, and some others

2.4.1 Reading about and describing architecture

To be asked what your favourite building is might be like asking a child for their favourite superhero. Like a film or song, there are too many to choose from and too many different genres. To split the favourite building question into a few typologies makes it easier. I find that distinctive styles of design, eras or even materials give different reactions of admiration, excitement, or respect of buildings. For example, your favourite house design will be never been able to compete with your favourite skyscraper, they are just so fundamentally different.

The architecture world is constantly replenishing. However, many buildings there are in the world, you will never have seen them all and therefore there is always something to learn. Buildings that sadly (or gladly) only ever stayed on the drawing board would make a brilliant architecture documentary. I am always happy to look up random buildings online, to experience that first split second of imagery and think 'wow that's incredible' or 'oh that's horrible'. It is like the ultimate architecture speed date. In a split-second moment you see a building and it hits your consciousness. Then on closer inspections you might change your mind or learn more about what the building actually does.

If you can think about your most and least favoured building, maybe the most important reasoning is that it made you feel something strongly. If you dislike it, make sure you know why. If you think it can be improved, make sure you could explain what it should be or how it can be designed in a different way. Anything that gets you a bit agitated about buildings is a good thing, like anything that provokes a response. There have been many buildings where I am amazed how bad it looks. How can a qualified architect seriously think that looks ok? It is good to be critical of the world, but I think you need to justify it. I am a big cynic anyway, I like to disbelieve things people say to me, I like to challenge what has been told to me.

It is important to speak up when you believe in something but listen intently when somebody else is making their point too. To give reason behind your strong opinions is vital. Career wise, I would say it is vital for pushing boundaries, showing that you care, and being the one who says, yes, I like it, but it could be even better. Your own thoughts can be your own education, understanding why you liked something when you first saw it but then from another angle changing your mind. Architecture thrives on humans pushing the boundaries and not being satisfied with the norm. It has resulted in some of the astonishing buildings I am about to discuss, so join the debate and get your architectural thinking going.

2.4.2 Describing architecture to a novice

I remember a good way of describing architecture to a novice, that I want to share. It was a 'beginners' architecture' lesson to a friend. He had worked in

197

television production most of his life, and had no idea and no care for architecture. I told him to first just look at a building, and imagine it as a person. I said, tell me what that person looks like to you, in building form. Just like when you make first impressions of people you meet, you can do that for buildings too. Aesthetics are still affecting your mind in the same way. Is the building big, small, friendly looking or threatening? Does it have stature and importance? Is it hard looking and serious, or soft and gentle? Maybe muscular, strong looking, dominant, and slightly scary? Does it welcome you in and look inviting, or is it private and confrontational? What does the façade say - is it obvious where you can 'interact' with the building? Maybe the entrance is hidden and confusing and you can't tell how to use this building. But maybe the entrance is clear, bright and engaging, like when you meet a pleasant smiling person. Are there balconies, terraces, changes of height, interesting or sharp shapes, ugly oversized parts? These features are all a good way to interpret the building and find out how it makes you feel.

When I started explaining more to him, I realised I was teaching myself a few angles too. A building could be magical and exciting, it could be serious or even sad, or thoughtful. Buildings can be nondescript and leave you feeling totally uninspired, much like some people do too. What is the design saying to the world from the architect's point of view? Is it a big statement of visual architecture? Is it a big gesture of geometry or pure size? This can be as much about the architect's style or ego as much as how they are trying to make the viewer of the building feel. Try looking at buildings through the viewpoint of what they do, or give, to the people around them.

2.4.3 My favourite buildings, and some others

Why are some buildings so famous? It's the location, the place, the buildings and their beauty. Those famous locations and buildings often really stand for something. They represent political achievements, societal movements, attitudes and the history on which they are based. For example, London, Rome or Paris are quite different to Cairo, Delhi or Kuala Lumpur for exactly those reasons. Every place is a product of its history and therefore it's people. They represent something far bigger than you think and are hugely influential. It's a good angle to consider this social responsibility side of architecture.

The buildings below are a list of my favourites, that anyone else could very easily compare with. I have visited them all and really admired them for different reasons. You could search them yourself and see what you think of them, either as a first impression or once you know a bit more. In a few years' time, you should have your own equivalent list.

Highbury Square (Arsenal Stadium - East Stand), London – 1913 Archibald Leitch.

This building used to be one side of a football stadium (that I visited hundreds of times), but was then preserved as part of an extensive residential refurbishment that I then worked on. It's only seen from the street elevation, unless you live within the residential complex where you can stand in the central garden, but that street view is the most impressive. It's art deco style, white renders stone, beautifully proportioned. The building looks very serene, very solid but still calm, and an example of an era of design where smooth pure facades were popular. It could easily be a historic town hall or museum if it were on a plaza. It has the important and regal style. It represents to me what a beautiful elevation can teach you about architecture. It looks smart, noble, upstanding, neat, classical, sensible, powerful but honest. You feel like you should behave well when you walk near this building.

Lord's Cricket Ground main stand,
London – 1889. Thomas Verity.

This classic cricket pavilion is a beautiful blend between a castle and a country mansion. The stone decoration is detailed and ornate, but even from far away you can feel the care and manual workmanship taken over every inch of the building. Its design is consistent and well balanced, and being on a cricket pitch that heightens the sense of symmetrical importance, but I think this building would look good anywhere. I love the lightness of the balcony railings, the proportion of floor levels and the proudly standing towers on either side.

Kings Cross St Pancras station,
London – 1868. WIlliam H Barlow.

One of my all-time favorites, it is so rich in decoration and history. Visually it is a Harry Potter style building. It stands for and exudes importance. I feel like I should be dressed well if I ever go past this building. I like the deep, classy colour, the size of the stone, the effort of detailing, and the scale and dominance of its surroundings. It looks dominant from far away to give an aura of importance, being proportionally perfect. The slight curve welcoming you to the courtyard is a grand entrance. Even inside, it's a dream combination of space, engineering, style and opulence. A visual reminder that old buildings should never ever be torn down.

Grand Central Station,
New York, USA – 1871. Whitney Warren.

I visited this station just once, and despite having seen various film scenes shot there, it still really blew me away with the same sort of historical importance as Kings Cross. I felt the history oozing out. This is not just a station, and is designed like that too. Why did the designer want a train station with a 4 stories high volume for the ticket lobby? Quite unnecessary functionally, but the design makes this space a stage. A space where the atmosphere feels far more than the basic function. I think you cannot appreciate its power unless standing inside. The light streaming in from those huge curved windows is amazing, scaled so big to give a feeling of importance. The building is more of an arrival 'moment' in NYC, and communicates that classic American attitude of being big, bold and patriotic.

Milan Cathedral,
Milan, Italy – began 1386. Simone da Orsenigo.

When I walked through the Galleria Vittorio opposite, and suddenly saw this giant façade appear on the left, it was a very rare moment of feeling genuinely astonished and slightly frightened. What an incredibly powerful and dominant, scary and spiritually commanding façade. It was far more textured than I thought, decorated in a way that is difficult to adequately describe. It is almost threatening, but so visually a place of God. This made me so aware of the power of religion and that underlying psychological meaning of what religions stand for. The big courtyard gives enough space to stand back in the presence of the dominant façade. Even just the triangular shape was powerful.

Cologne cathedral,
Cologne, Germany – began 1248. Unknown.

Similarly, to the gothic style of Milan Cathedral, it is astonishing how human beings made this building. Even now the construction would be a challenge, but being so long ago through bare hands and communication is a great lesson in itself. The size, shape and scale look so perfectly balanced. The visual weight and solidity of it looks too big for humans. What an amazing difference between these buildings compared to what we produce now. When religion dominated life, it shows what people valued and needed for meaning and belief.

Houses of Parliament,
London – began 1840. Augustus Pugin. William Barry.

Another fairly easy choice along the stunning Gothic lines, but an all-time favorite for its calmness, authority and regal beauty, whilst being powerful in its shape and dominance of the location. It forms a perfect combination with the riverside site, the large black gates, Big Ben, being the center of London. It's a perfect night time silhouette.

Metropolitan Cathedral,

Rio de Janeiro, Brazil – 1964. Edgar de Oliveira da Fonseca.

This was an amazing find that I had never seen or heard of before it emerged around the corner on my journey. It is a pyramid church that seems very underused, despite its visual and logical enclosure a space. But it is spoilt by its dirty and strange surroundings. The façade is created from boxed, gridded modular panels, that give an interesting façade. Then when stepping inside, it felt lonely. It is hard, quiet, and cold but from the religious point of view, gives security, faith, and protection. A fascinating design.

Intercontinental Hotel,
Melbourne, Australia – 1980. WIlliam Pitt.

This hotel has a facade style and richness of design you will find in many global cities but this one is a great example of perfect façade lighting. It is wedged between others on a fairly tight Melbourne CBD Street. I like this one because it's less of a building and more of a feeling given by design. It exudes class and wealth. The lighting, the tones of material, and the warmness of it looks cozy, welcoming and cared for, still crucial design elements to a city hotel.

Al Ibrahimi building,
Abu Dhabi, UAE – 1983. Farouk El Gohary. (unconfirmed).

I had to search hard to even find the name, as this building is not really known apart from those who live next to it, or helped design it. The appearance of the locale around it, tells you it is a gem of a building, but in an untidy, disorderly lost city street. It is a cool yet simply repeated design, almost parametric, which experiments with scale, hence the great imagination of the modular pattern. Perhaps it took biophilic inspiration with its organic style. A circular floor plate is not common, but the façade repetition is very natural and fluid to me. The design could be modelled directly from a structure of bacteria or biology. Purely the shape and unusual effect make this a memorable building to me.

Hotel Inglaterra, and Havana overall,
Cuba – 1875. Manuel Lopez.

This choice partly represents the whole of the city (and most of Cuba probably) as a stunning mixture of architecture, as worrying as it is encapsulating. The city has a slightly dystopian and edgy style. Generally, a colonial almost beautiful gothic style yet so crooked and dangerous that each building looks like a frail old man with a walking stick. Hotel Inglaterra sits majestically on the city plaza and would probably be ignored if it were on a tight street. It's iconic in Havana and represents the history of the place so much more. The interior has small square floor tiles, dark wood furniture and a film-set type décor. It really makes you feel like you've gone back a few decades.

Boston Public Library,
Boston, USA – 1895. Charles Follen McKim.

The classic library scene is probably romanticized in films and American tv, but those glorious high ceiling rooms, with arched windows letting in rays of light, and small green lampshades on expensive looking desks gives a homely secure feeling. There always seems to be a few people sitting, studying or writing. This library interior design style has almost become famous in its own right. The corridors leading to this room are gorgeous too, perfectly finished and giving that sense of intelligence and importance.

Casa Mila,
Barcelona, Spain – 1912. Antonio Gaudi.

Definitely one to study as a historical moment sticking out like a sore thumb. In an age where nothing like it was considered, anywhere in the world, Guadi made some astonishing statements. It's progressive, imaginative architecture but quite divisive in opinions that I have heard. I like the playful and theatrical nature of the curves, and links effortlessly to Barcelona's style. I don't think it was replicated for many hundreds of years until fluid smooth design came along again in the past couple of decades. How did this style survive so long yet be so rarely replicated? Read a few minutes about Guadi's design influence and tragic death, it is quite a story.

Guggenheim Museum,
Bilbao, Spain – 1997. Frank Gehry.

This wildly freestyle spaceship form is not really my sort of design style overall, but it is the ingenuity and imagination that I can really admire. It's such a strange jumble, yet somehow sits quite serenely next to the river. How you the human mind create such a design is beyond me. Maybe a load of plasticine, clay, or foil models, creating a twisted wreckage of recycled metal parts. How ever it was done, Gehry made an astonishing statement to the world. He is quite a compelling guy to listen to if you can find his online interviews. I think it's one of those buildings massively helped by its site location. You can get such a good look at it from many angles. Often magnificent buildings on a tight high street never quite get recognized because you cannot stand back and admire it. Sitting across the river in Bilbao is perfectly situated. How does such a crazy object make you feel about design? Could this style only be a museum typology? Or could anything like that be a residential block? Wouldn't it be cool if that was your school or college? Amazing use of materials too, I think it's pushes boundaries of architecture.

The Eden Project,
Cornwall, UK – 2000. Tim Smit and Nicholas Grimshaw.

I love this building because it is visually an architectural, structural, and engineering marvel all together. The form shows how it works and gives so many lessons. It makes me wonder why so many buildings are just square blocks? Circular or spherical design is so pure and so inherently pleasing but rarely used. Eden project matches the brief and the result so well, again with an amazing site to help it. It is superbly detailed, inspiring and challenges what architecture can do. Also check out 'Biosphere 2', an amazing sustainability experiment conducted in America in the 80s, well worth 5 minutes reading.

Merchandise Mart,
Chicago, USA – 1930. Ernest Graham.

I choose this one for a single reason, scale. At the time it was the world largest building by pure size. Maybe it was the angle I saw it from, or the expansive never-ending façade, but the size and proportions just struck me when I first saw it. Scale is a crucial weapon of design to understand, and this building did it for me. Retaining the human scale at floor level, but stretching the windows on the façade, it is also the vertical strength and towering bookends that look absolutely monstrous. Utterly awesome like a wall of solid cladding. But also beautifully positioned and balanced. I like the proportions between each floor, the cornice, then the long stretch of vertical windows towards the solid roof. If this standing by itself and more isolated, I think it would be world famous. It makes my mind wonder what we have done to this planet, to need such whopping buildings, all for the purpose of merchandise and shopping.

1111 Lincoln Road,
Miami, USA (and Beirut Terraces, Lebanon) – 2008.
Herzog de Mueron.

Seeing both of these similar designs in the flesh was exciting, and both communicate the simplicity of architecture, building and living. They are just flat slab levels, stacked, where people live or use the space. It exudes the sort of design simplicity where you wonder why you had not thought of that. It relies on calculated, balanced and controlled design, resulting in simple proportion and purity. It shows structure being used as design theory in such a good way. A building that makes me just want to sit there and draw it.

Dusseldorf residences,
Dusseldorf, Germany – 1998. Frank Gehry.

Buildings generally aren't designed with angular, jagged, irregular, uneven facades or levels, it is just far too inefficient. But designs such as this challenge that and show it to be worthy. Gehry brought that to the table, and it just works in harmony despite its fractured sharp style. Also, worth seeing Gehry's residential tower in NYC, crinkled stainless steel panels, creating an amazing effect. Why don't more architects excite and thrill and shake life up a bit with such twisted abstract shapes? I guess it comes down to money and efficiency a lot of the time, but this is famously a Gehry style and so recognizable. It is like he invented a shape. How amazing is that. Also search the Stata Centre, at MIT in Boston.

Prudential Tower,
Chicago, USA – 1974. Edward Durell Stone. Perkins & W.

Not a world-famous building and you might not be impressed to look it up, but in my earlier years when I visited, it challenged my understanding of design. The simple and perhaps boring nature of this super long tower makes me look at it more than any other boring tower. The absolute resolute addiction to straight lines all the way up building, without interruption, makes this strangely interesting, more so when you realise it needs mechanical plant level vents or grilles. If you are looking for a pure monolith statement of design, is there anything wrong with this level of simplicity? I can see now that if the façade was ever interrupted, it would spoil the entire concept. The pure white helps, but it is the deliberate rigid façade design that it interests me.

Bank of America,
Miami, USA – 1987. IM Pei.

Similarly, above, this is not such a 'favourite' but more of an example I want to highlight. I went here and was just amazed by the simplicity of the design approach. What are you saying to the world with your building design? What does this building say to you? How can such a huge important building be so simple and bland? Why only the horizontal lines? Eventually the answer came to me, that the design is saying I'm a serious building, I don't need to look nice. I am a functional, financial, business building and I don't want to show anything about me except that I am strong and immovable. The building looks like such a huge block of stone, almost like it's been there for thousands of years. My lesson was that designing facades in an 'additive' way is powerful, but perhaps taking some of that design away and seeing what you are left with, can be quite powerful too.

The Icon Tower,
Melbourne, Australia – 2015. JCB Architects.

A fun, colourful, interesting and playful building, it's pretty much like children's coloured building blocks stacked up, slightly off alignment. I have heard other colleagues say they hate it, but I quite like its lesson in architecture. Literally, it's building with blocks. They stack, not quite in line, whilst still looking interesting. What would a city look like if it were all this colourful? Well cities don't, so maybe this is why you can design with colour.

Also, you must look at Hotel Zandaam. A crazy, childish, but completely unique interpretation of a building, you really must see it.

Bahrain Towers,
Manama, Bahrain – 2008. Killa Design.

A very eye catching and imaginative design, which clearly tries to tell you what is happening with the huge turbines spinning between two towers. A perfect visualization of clean energy production and how buildings should be contributing to their environment and the world. It's a futuristic shape with a design language telling you what is happening and what the design is doing. I like it, but I am not sure it works in the way it shows it does. Some headlines are not so positive about it.

Al Bahr Towers,
Abu Dhabi, UAE – 2012. AHR Architects.

Often named the 'pineapple towers' in Abu Dhabi, I think this sort of concept is the future of architecture, much like the Killa Tower above. I see buildings being changeable, moveable, and interactive. If you create energy sustainably, that is a perfect solution to harsh climates. As a design and educational statement, it pushes boundaries and creating something different. It is a highly describable building, which is often what you want from a statement design that makes you learn as you look at it. The partially opened and closed shading panels give even the most non-architectural people a fair clue as to what is happening.

Capital Gate building,
Abu Dhabi, UAE – 2011. RMJM.

A brilliant innovation of compressible blockwork being used to bend back into shape during building process. It is like a leaning flower or tree. A great concept, well finished, and another wow factor building that would not be conceivable a few years ago. The silhouette grabs your attention and I think makes you interested about the structural engineering. So, rewarding the ingenuity is crucial. How can an architect ever come up with new ideas when such buildings occur? Also see the twisting building in Dubai Marina.

Valencia Science City,
Valencia, Spain – 1998. Santiago Calatrava.

Visually like nothing I had ever seen before, with astonishing imagination to think of shapes and combinations. The 3D software available now was only in infancy through this design, but it's come out incredibly well. A great example of educating and exciting society with design. Anyone must be attracted to look at it and wonder. Strangely the buildings are slightly tatty around the edges, but the area is popular because of the architecture, and should have people buzzing around it all day. It's like seeing the Star Wars cities in real life, or a futuristic bike helmet.

Habitat housing,
Montreal, Canada – 1967. Moshe Safdie.

A building in this list that I haven't actually been to close up, but only seen from afar whilst looking down the hill to the marina in Montreal. But this residential project is absolutely worth studying on so many levels. There are a few examples that Safdie applied around the world, and the typology has been adopted in many offshoot designs. The initial appearance and wow factor is great, but behind it lies interesting ideas for communal living. Is it what you want from clustered blocks of residential apartments? Certainly ground breaking at the time and seen as very progressive. The challenge for dense urban living is changing all the time, and this was a fascinating contribution to it. Would you want to live here?

Chand Baori,
Rajasthan, India. 8th Century. (unknown)

One last bit of indulgence of a building I have not visited, but such an alternative interpretation of reality. I feel like this could be a future world or a computer game, but the design was actually made exactly this way for convenience and ease of use. I am fascinated with what designers sometimes produce It makes me enjoy what architecture and design can be in terms of satisfying a brief. I have chosen this one because it shows, in the same way to designing an office, house, or museum, your concept design can and should be absolutely individually based on your interpretation, not needing to be like anything ever done before. This is innovation, even though it was thousands of years ago.

For a few indulgent minutes, I have some Milton Keynes equivalents to write about, purely for the joy of assessing this bizarre concrete metropolis which I grew up in. It's quite an odd place. But at the same time, I think Milton Keynes is hugely underestimated for its place in British architectural history, theory and planning strategy. It's kind of lost between what the architectural world could be, or should be, but also what it really shouldn't be. The city always had some bad press, but hopefully the following will provide some interesting analysis.

Milton Keynes Central Train station,
Milton Keynes, UK – 1982. Stuart Mosscrop.

The sort of forgotten, misunderstood and unfortunate building that to me, is of a huge significance and should be celebrated and studied. If it were the train station of a visited capital city, it would be world famous. But the Milton Keynes train station has no sense of place, so it is forgotten. When modernism took hold, I think simplicity and purity was at the heart of it. So this example is a blue glass expanse of Mies van der Rohe inspired modernism. It represents balance and solidity and shows no complications about how a building can be designed. There is a certain perfection to it, of simple geometry and rectangular, angular repetition. The huge unused expanse of concrete in front of the building really gives you no reason to stop and admire the architecture. Would you take a photo here when you get out of the station? The top of the building could be a spectacular viewpoint, with a restaurant or bar looking directly up Midsummer Boulevard. The two bridges either side do not really celebrate the linked nature of MK, do not show off where you can go next, or where you can walk to.

There have been recent moves to develop it into commuter focused apartments, but over the years it has been badly underused as generic office space. For many thousands of commuters and visitors per year, this is the introduction to Milton Keynes. A soulless expanse of concrete and a painful letdown to any visitor the to the city. It feels miles away from where visitors thought the MKC train station would leave them. The reality is that many people take an onward journey in a car, bus or taxi from that point, which often contradicts the very advantage of any train station being central.

The main shopping center (and therefore main reason why many thousands of people go to MK), is actually a 30 minutes' walk up-hill to Midsummer Place. This shows an amazing lack of forethought for how the city might operate in reality. The columns coming down to ground level on each side of the plaza could form a stylish and well protected arcade if there was any reason to actually stroll round them and visit cafes or small shops. Now it results in low price substandard goods where nobody would want to walk for lack of public safety let along enjoyment. The actual plaza area has weeds growing though the wonky and broken paving stones, two bland grass lawns and some flag poles with no flags. Such a good-sized public square should be hosting food fairs, craft events, or music concerts through the summer weekends, or open markets. But there is nothing to admire here, nothing to stop for, nothing to read or learn about.

The Xscape Ski dome,
Milton Keynes, UK – 2000. Future Systems

I was a teenager living in MK when this headline modernist project was going up. Big ideas, big shape, a big economic stimulus and the success should supposedly radiate out from there. The problem is, I think it's just a bit big and ugly. It's almost more grey than I can ever imagine. The monotone insulated panels are so grey I can hardly imagine what colour is anymore. The huge domineering curved hemisphere is visible from so far around it's an absolute beast on the horizon, and difficult to miss, considering all of MK was restricted to 6 storey for the first 30 years of its development. I would advise you to look from a Google earth aerial view instead of the front elevation. The elevation doesn't really celebrate the purity of the arch as well as it could.

The Point (multiplex cinema),
Milton Keynes, UK - 1985. Building Design Partnership.

In the 1980s this was one of the most recognizable buildings to MK residents. It was loosely an entertainment zone, with arcade games, video games and a cinema. It's quite an amazing design in terms of shape an imagination. It's technically a ziggurat. Effectively a pyramid, with 3 levels made up of huge glass boxes, with a smaller and smaller footprint for each level up. It has very reflective glass and a striking red pyramid truss which attaches at the corner of each glass block. It's an astonishing design that deserves more attention. It would fit in well on the Las Vegas strip, but there is something horribly awkward about its mirror glass facade, awful signage, and poor entrance experience. At night time the bright red neon lights gave it a certain allure, but only because I was 10 years old and thought it looked cool.

My overall thought is 'what were you thinking?' And I don't mean that critically, but honestly what were the designers trying to produce with this incredible shape?

Utterly interesting and captivating, but maybe creates more questions than answers.

Milton Keynes Shopping center,
Milton Keynes, UK - 1979. MKDC.

The shopping center is nearly a mile long and an icon of MK. It was a catalyst for all-in-one indoor shopping centres that undeniably revolutionized shopping and retail in the UK. Technically based on Mies van der Rohe designs and purity of shape and geometry, much like the MK train center described above. The shopping center is genuinely a nice place to be. Its slim ceiling and cladding profiles let in so much light and provide the right level of shelter at the same time as airy external vibe. It's like a huge conservatory shaped as an 'H' from above. Shops lined every avenue and are almost continuously filled. It's always clean, always busy and formed a reliable hub for everything you could possibly need.

From the design point of view, it is an ingenious arrangement of all deliveries coming in from roof level, thus leaving the entire perimeter free of relentless delivery vans and excess traffic. In summary, much loved and always busy, a modern interpretation from the traditional city centre hub around square or plaza.

Bletchley Leisure Center,
Milton Keynes, UK - 1974. Faulkner Browns Architects

This is a very obscure one, and yet another pyramid. It was a beacon for MK residents, with good urban interaction and a cool sense of arrival as you came round the gradual curved road on approach. It was basically a big glass pyramid, with a swimming pool inside. Simple as that. For the whole of my childhood, it was one of the fondest and most exciting memories. It represented not only fun swimming lessons, but a happy day out. If you are ever lucky enough to meet someone from Milton Keynes of around my age, I'm sure they will remember the amazing Bletchley swimming pool. This building communicates memories as much as architecture to me, which is a powerful thing. The emotion of the building becomes stronger than the bricks and mortar itself. It is similar in scale to the pyramids at Giza in Egypt, or the Louvre in Paris. They are cherished around the world, representing mankind's most astonishing accomplishment. But this glass pyramid swimming pool in Bletchley was a battered old relic really. Sadly, it was replaced with a new bland, boring, modernist aluminum clad box design, which contained, hilariously, a swimming pool.

What I learnt from my first few years of really travelling and seeing some of the world's most celebrated architecture, is that cities and countries become the travel wishes of millions, for very simple reasons. People want to go to Barcelona because of the Sagrada Familia, or the New York 'skyline' walk, or the Burj Khalifa in Dubai, or the Christ Redeemer Statue in Rio. I personally wanted to visit the world's biggest stadiums. People spend thousands of pounds to fly round the world to visit these places, mostly because they showcase successful cities and impressive buildings. And it is not always for the design of it, but what it represents. Think of Buckingham Palace, it's not an amazing design really, but globally famous as soon as you see it.

For an opposite angle on the above descriptions, below are a few similarly famous buildings that for some reason I've just never been that impressed by:

Sydney Opera House,
Sydney, Australia – 1973. Jorg Utson.

I know it is an absolute icon of Sydney and Australia with its stunning shape instantly recognizable silhouette, and being more than just a building but a symbol. For some reason I find it quite awkward. I have seen it up close and it was dirty, the detailing at each 'crease' looked a little shabby, and it's not quite as pure and light as it looks. Clearly an amazing building, but maybe like a good film, I've just seen it too many times.

Sagrada Familia,
Barcelona, Spain – began 1882. Antonio Gaudi.

I'm sure this will be another unpopular opinion to you, but whilst I can appreciate it is an amazing piece of work to build so tall for a start, so much of it looks like an unbalanced melted candle. I have never quite understood why fruits are hanging from the spires of this church, it just does not quite compute to me. Maybe I expect church or religious architecture to be more symmetrical. It's fascinating for sure, but with building work, tower cranes and protective covers always obscuring the true building, I can't really appreciate the powerful church typology that is probably hidden underneath.

Le Corb Notre Dame de Haut,
Paris, France – 1955. Le Corbusier.

This appears in nearly every architecture theory book, but I have just never got it. Odd shape, ugly looking, out of scale, more of a sculpture, with stark white render. It looks distorted, like it has been elongated incorrectly. This is commonly used in university education but not somewhere I would want to visit, let alone live. The roof is ridiculous, looks like thatch from a distance away and weird shape like a hat. I don't like the proportion or size and it doesn't look welcoming. It must be famous because of Le Corbusier, but by any other architect I don't think it would hold much influence.

The White House,
Washington DC, USA – 1792. James Hoban.

Maybe one of the most famous buildings in the world, but not architecturally special in any way as far as I can see. It just happens to be the house of the most powerful man in the world. The architectural atmosphere, style and design is of a certain time and looks kind of nice, but does not have anything special about it. There are probably thousands of buildings like that around the world, in fact many big American houses out in the very wealthy suburbs looks very similar with their thick white columns and balanced classical style, but just not that amazing.

Selfridges,
Birmingham UK – 1999. Future Sytems.

This building was massive news in the UK at the time, and I can see the amazing contrast with the historical church right next to it. But overall, it's just a big blob. I don't like buildings when I cannot really describe them very well. Maybe I feel like you need to put more effort into a building for it to be worthy, and this one is just a bit simple, odd and awkward. Conceptually fascinating, and perhaps it works really well inside, or has ingenious functionality that I don't know about. It was crucial for Birmingham's regeneration and arguably made a big positive impact on that city, but it is just not for me.

2.5 FAMOUS ARCHITECTURAL QUOTES

Millions of architectural quotes, phrases and sentences have been uttered, written, celebrated or perhaps forgotten over the years, and some wise words never had the exposure to the world. An amazing quote I remember hearing, yet cannot quite place, goes something like - "architecture is simply when you are not outside". It's a bit simplistic, but actually fundamentally true and descriptive when you think about it. You could be sitting in the ugliest and most uncomfortable space or room, but it's still a building that somewhere along the line was designed by a human being, and therefore it's architecture.

I have also heard the phrase that history is only one side of the story, and is only written by those alive to describe what happened. I think architecture is often a reflection of that, and a reflection of the time in which it was produced, so it's links to society and politics are very strong. I think architecture quotes are very similar. Some will not resonate with you, some will enlighten you, and some may confuse you, then you'll probably be able to think up a few of your own.

"Simplicity is the ultimate sophistication."
Leonardo da Vinci

"I think you never stop learning."
Norman Foster

"Recognizing the need is the primary condition for design."
Charles Eames

"Architecture is really about well-being. On the one hand it's about shelter, I think that people want to feel good in a space... but it's also about pleasure."
Zaha Hadid

"I don't think that architecture is only about shelter... it should be able to excite you, to calm you, to make you think."
Zaha Hadid

"Architecture is about people."
Francis Kere

"Regard it as just as desirable to build a chicken house as to build a cathedral."
Frank Lloyd Wright

"There are no straight lines or sharp corners in nature. Therefore, buildings must have no straight lines or sharp corners"
Antonio Gaudi

"I believe that architecture, as anything else in life, is evolutionary. Ideas evolve; they don't come from outer space and crash into the drawing board." Bjarke Ingels

"The one thing all humans share is that we all inhabit the same limited amount of real estate, which is Planet Earth." Bjarke Ingels

"A kid in Minecraft can build a world and inhabit it through play. We have the possibility to build the world

that we want to inhabit."
Bjarke Ingels

"I see my buildings as pieces of cities, and in my designs, I try to make them into responsible and contributing citizens." César Pelli

"Layering and changeability: this is the key, the combination that is worked into most of my buildings. Occupying one of these buildings is like sailing a yacht; you modify and manipulate its form and skin according to seasonal conditions and natural elements, and work with these to maximize the performance of the building."
Glenn Murcutt

"Architecture is a learned game, correct and magnificent, of forms assembled in the light."
Le Corbusier

"I prefer drawing to talking. Drawing is faster, and leaves less room for lies."
Le Corbusier

"As an architect you design for the present, with an awareness of the past, for a future which is essentially unknown."
Norman Foster

"Architecture is an expression of values."
Norman Foster

"Architects work in two ways. One is to respond precisely to a client's needs or demands. Another is to look

at what the client asks and reinterpret it."
  Rem Koolhaas

*"The speed of change makes you wonder what will
become of architecture."*
  Tadao Ando

"People ignore design that ignores people."
Frank Chimero

*"Good design is all about making other designers feel
like idiots because the idea wasn't theirs."*
  Frank Chimero

*"In pure architecture the smallest detail should have a
meaning or serve a purpose."*
  Augustus W. N. Pugin

"Design is where science and art break even."
Mieke Gerritzen

*"Architecture arouses sentiments in man. The
architect's task, therefore, is to make those sentiments
more precise"*
  Adolf Loos

*"The greatest architectural illusion is not Baroque fancy
or Victorian flamboyant, but minimalism."*
  Kevin McCloud

*"When I'm working on a problem, I never think about
beauty. But when I'm finished, if the solution is not
beautiful, I know it's wrong"*

Buckminster Fuller

"I call architecture frozen music"
Johann Wolfgang von Goethe

"Any work of architecture that does not express serenity is a mistake"
Luis Barragán

"I don't know why people hire architects and then tell them what to do"
Frank Gehry

"Architecture is inhabited sculpture"
Constantin Brancusi

"The architect's role is to make the mythic real."
Sotirios Kotoulas

"Architecture is like a mythical fantastic. It has to be experienced. It can't be described. We can draw it up and we can make models of it, but it can only be experienced as a complete whole"
Maya Lin

"It's a very complicated process to do large projects. You start to see the society, how it functions, how it works. Then you have a lot of criticism about how it works"
Ai Weiwei

"Recognizing the need is the primary condition for design."
Charles Eames.

"You employ stone, wood and concrete, and with these materials you build houses and palaces. That is construction. Ingenuity is at work. But suddenly you touch my heart, you do me good, I am happy and I say: This is beautiful. That is Architecture. Art enters in."
Le Corbusier.

"Difficult details lead to construction knowledge, which leads to knowledge of constructing difficult details"
Joe Healey.

2.6 CONSIDERING THE ARCHITECTURAL FUTURE

Change in the architecture industry is quite gradual. It's quite slow when you analyse it. I like the chance to look forward a couple of generations and to discuss what the industry will look like. Seeing the developments of the past five or ten years have given me some ideas, but I'm sure there's going to be some even more crazy innovations just round the corner.

I think it's interesting to see architecture as a mirror of history. By that I mean buildings mold and shape human existence because they control how we use places. What we build defines who we are, what we can do, and how we can do it. But who we are, and what we can do, defines what we can build. It is a very cultural and philosophical subject, and can always tell you about the success or failures of a place dependent on its architecture.

Architecture in 10 years

I think predicting the future can be quite well informed by the past. To analyse the state of the architectural industry every ten years from the 1950s would show an astonishing change. Technology is really out of control in some ways. We are using technology so fast and with such eagerness, I sometimes feel like we're not stopping to check whether it is for the overall good. For that reason, I wonder whether historical and valuable heritage buildings will be more at risk of redevelopment, either through not having enough people to appreciate it, or there's not enough benefit to a city or town to justify it against huge investment and profitable development.

Taking churches as a great example where I grew up in the UK. Churches are magnificent, powerful, emotive structures, obviously very old but quite trusted and valuable to the community. In many westernized cities, churches really do not hold anything like the influence they used to, so perhaps their value decreases. For example, if 20% of a town's inhabitants visit a church each week, but then in ten years' time that number is down to 5%, there will be less and less justification to keep the building. It is tough to think about, but if churches are less and less relevant, there will be less and less people to fight for its retention and educational benefit. Development should always serve the people that live around it.

It is a really interesting angle to discuss architecture potentially designing out entire industries. For example, will passenger lifts ever become so common that you never need to take a flight of stairs anymore? Omitting stairs completely would save a lot of valuable space in tower buildings, for example. If emergency escape methods become advanced enough, fire safety and strategy could be completely changed. Simply from a domestic convenience and safety point of view, a lift is much better than stairs.

For a separate example, will the negative environmental impact of mixing concrete finally make designers and developers stop using it altogether? Its water usage is huge and similar outcomes can be achieved with other structural materials. On a wider scale of change, has the development of online shopping and delivery convenience caused the disappearance of shopping centers or retail parks? Their design has certainly changed in recent years in line with demand and combination with entertainment or social spaces to allow an all-day shopping sort of experience.

One change I particularly acknowledge, is that if buildings become better at absorbing, collecting and storing their own energy, will they still need to be connected at district level to vast gas pipes, generators and electricity supplies, with all the associated underground work? That's a big saving in excavation cost and disturbance of local wildlife. A building could be truly self-sufficient if it produces and then uses all the energy it needs right there within it's footprint.

It's probably best to start with the immediate changes I am seeing in the industry. This is just my experience, so it is good to make similar assessments yourself and identify patterns you see emerging.

Projects

In terms of the day-to-day role, I can see the gradual slimming down and further diluting of an architecture professional's role. In a few years, qualified architects might be more solely 'concept' architects. Architectural technicians and technologists' input would have improved and partly combined with engineers and designers. That group will hold most of the building knowledge in terms of coordination and construction, so the concept will sit a little more detached from that. The industry has more separated roles as discussed previously, but this is less centered on the architect. Conceptual architecture utilizes stunning software effects and uses more computational designs now to create incredible, exciting building geometry. That powerful level of software usage will carve out its own niche for some companies to concentrate on.

There still seems to be lots of value in producing

stunning architectural concept images. The problem is they are often quite unachievable in reality, so the actual knowledge for constructing these designs will be paramount to project success. In some ways, you could say anyone can have a great vision, as many people do, but to turn it into reality is where the real difference lies. So, I think project knowledge and hands-on construction expertise will become highly sought after.

This improved digital output means better reusing, repurposing, and recycling of previous designs, multiplying efficiency of the concept stage. For example, a company's previous projects are saved in such a usable way in terms of data, models and drawings, that it doesn't take much to present that in a completely different project with subtle changes. If a developer wants an identical building size and floor plate to a development they procured 5 years ago, how acceptable is it to fully recycle a previous project from the architects' archives, but simply give it a slightly different façade dimension? The reliable library of previous designs that architects have is hugely valuable to clients, allowing immediate calculation of total floor space, areas and volumes, quickly changing between infinite design options. The people who can punch out those designs will be invaluable.

Production

Schedules and project programmes are now tighter than ever, and whether you agree with that trend or not, I think the industry has brought it on. The project timeline has become crunched more and more over the years, because the design is theoretically easier to do. There is more work and more deliverables to complete than historically, but I think those deliverables are easier to produce now. Flexibility and adaptability are massive. Looking back, when I was comparing and drawing AutoCAD floor plans and sections, copying and moving construction lines with aligned overlays, it was really basic and risky for discrepancies. The 3D world of BIM has allowed massive strides forward, which impacts client's perception of design speed. Costs are continually pinched, because authority approval or permitting stages are now overlapping with design stage, and design stage is overlapping on-site construction. That's natural in my view. In any industry, things always have to be done a little cheaper, a little quicker, a little more efficiently. It is natural progression for humans in any industry really. Computer power and software innovation has allowed us to do that. We are constantly innovating, but becoming frustrated when that innovation brings new possibilities that need us to work harder.

If you consider architecture as a version of manufacturing or production, I certainly think flat-pack and modular building will increase hugely, in the same way that flat pack furniture and flexible home or office spaces have. Architecture in terms of construction processes can be heavily automated. Not only in products and building elements, but also the improvement and adaptation of the building process. Optimum design can be calculated by models, whilst manufacture and construction can be controlled by machines. I think this will only increase for the next couple of decades, so the knowledge behind programming the computer output will become hugely valuable. My prediction is that you will have a more separated concept architect working independently, with 4 or 5 programmers and algorithm experts to draw out that imagination into reality.

Design imagination skills are under threat too from computers. Programming and coding allow feeding in parameters and boundaries to then automatically generate endless possible outcomes. It is just working out ways in which to satisfy the variables. You set the framework and get numerous versions of what can be realised with some amazing software. Imagination is still key for architectural designers, because we are still finding new interpretations of design, but can we still imagine new ways to construct the buildings too?

So, what is the architect's skill now? I think part of BIM modelling will also become automated. I have used Revit for many years now and even the most basic of design rules and model algorithms are used quite rarely in my experience. For a practical example, doors being pre-set to load in the right place according to regulations, pushing other items proportionally away from the door jamb or swing if there is not enough room, is an easy model attribute. Similarly, all doors can be placed 150mm from a nib, or with 300mm clear space from the swing edge. Formulas can be built in to the Revit families in a variety of applications, so that the model changes things automatically based on set parameters. Manufacturer model objects might pre-load how the object is fixed and what clearances are required, so the modelling skill and knowledge is taken away. Like when loading in an Accessible WC layout, you no longer need to design that because of the rigid regulation dimensions, so the principle of this computer led design will increase.

For working practices, I think shorter contract, temporary positions and maybe being hired on hour-by-hour basis, will become common. Companies may want to hire you as and when needed, because working time and skills will be flexible and agile. Maybe companies will have fewer full-time trusted employees, as a core group, then pay a little extra for specific skills at pinch points in the project. Using the exact skills at the exact time, for extreme efficiency. Again, taking a lesson from the past to see the future, employees used to stay with one or two companies for their whole life, but now it is so diverse how many countries, companies, and roles you can and will have.

Technology

I think before the end of this decade, it will be completely normal to put on a headset, grab the handle controls and walk your way round your project, either in design stage or for inspections. Perhaps your hologram client (or avatar) can be walking next to you, discussing parts of the building as you both look around. The technology is very exciting for cameras recording users' movements, transposing them to the model environment where they might stand next to each other and point out amendments. Imagine a site visit when you don't even go to site?

I think automated construction will become dominant too. Brick laying robots and pavement printing rollers are simple versions. Humans might become only supervision staff if the construction computer picks up QR coded parts and lifts them to preset heights for another computer arm to do the welding. Not good for the construction workers. A good example being modular construction. There are many interesting YouTube videos or documentaries showing factory production lines, or an Amazon warehouse scene, with an incredible level of automation.

Construction jobs will disappear because a machine can do it faster, more accurately and crucially, cheaper. Can you position yourself and your skills beyond what a machine can do?

I think 'multi-disciplinary' firms could become dominant. These are typically large construction and contractor orientated firms, where you have various architectural staff working alongside engineers like structural, MEP or hydraulic. It should be a far more efficient way of coordinating design. All the necessary skills are at your fingertips in one room, plus the client only has one company to deal with in terms of design, payments and contracts. These things go in cycles, so as soon as lots of multi-disciplinary companies start to dominate, contracts might spread the risk again, and tap into more specific skills that are particular to a company. I'm really interested to see where this will go.

I think the logical progression of specifications is; from hundreds of pages of A4 paper as it is currently, then to a divided set of independent works packages, to a diagrammatically connected online database of clauses that are directly linked to the model itself, in the future. An ever more screen-orientated industry will result in specification clauses popping-out as an info box when you click on the object in the model. That will tell you what product, what size, what colour, and click on the installation instructions, which come direct from the supplier website. The manufacturer and regulation writers combine their information, so the architect acts like a kind of translator of expertise, which further strips down their role. All industries change and adapt and can become obsolete, so the challenge is to be ready for them and know how to react if it happens.

Architecture in 20 years

Movement

Architectural futures as shown in films really resonate with me. Somewhere as simple as Star Wars or sci-fi films have predicted our 2050s future incredibly well. I particularly like the potential movement between super tall buildings, posing a question I considered a few years ago whilst visiting Hong Kong; could we live several days or weeks without touching the ground? Looking at skylines like Dubai, New York, Tokyo or Singapore, those towers could be connected by airport style horizontal moving walkways, or monorail lanes all controlled by computer adjustment of the height, trajectory, and altitude for vehicles. It is a reality not far away from the driverless cars boom of recent years. How will design of buildings and spaces get us there? The concept might be clear, but actual usable places will still need the refinement that architecture professionals can give.

Why go out of your apartment, down 30 floors in the lift, walk 10 meters across the street, just to go 30 floors up again in a lift? Theoretically, living several weeks at your level 30 apartment could be done, using sky gardens and shopping facilities at various levels of the tower, then working from home, getting your fresh air and environmental fix from the roof garden. Could you go months without ever having to go to ground level? What are the ramifications for the design of ground level if less and less people go there? I wrote my architectural studies dissertation in 2005 about the UK approach to post-war building 'streets in the sky'. Heavy density, low quality housing blocks were connected at high level by hard concrete bridge corridors. This was mistakenly assumed to be suitable for families, and soon became dangerously unhealthy.

Transport, movement and occupancy has been drastically affected since the Covid-19 pandemic struck. I think drone delivery expansion seems absolute inevitable, thus reducing the need for shopping in person, whether it be supermarkets or household items or clothes. Why go clothes shopping when a drone will fly it to you, to try on, and then you decide to keep it, or put it back in the drone to return? This will mean far less design requirement for the commercial sector.

Optimisation

Standardization is already massive in terms of company efficiency and automation of repeated designs, but also underused. There is an interesting situation ahead, where a commonly used building element with some exact features, like a standard masonry brick wall for example, would nationally, or maybe internationally, be forever known as a consistent coded type, for example BW01. If a trusted list of common building objects exists, companies could operate on the same classification data, so that eventually a whole district, region or country knows there are 15 standard wall types that never, ever, need to be redesigned, renamed or recoded. You just pick out which ones you need for the current project. This helps the project team in terms of identification, and also replacement or maintenance issues. Certainly, a vastly faster design process. You are simply trying to limit how many times to reinvent the wheel by agreeing on some repeated factors that never need to change.

Disease control and therefore overall surveillance of your movements could massively reduce what you can do with your life, and whether it's permitted by the state. There is obviously more health and cleanliness focus now, with touchless technology and individual bio-recognition on the way. Individual settings and personalisation of devices is common, so I wonder is the next step to rearrange your apartment furniture when a home computer identifies you about to enter? Plenty of that happens already like pre-set heating or garage doors opening on approach. Does that bring about new possibilities for flexible changeable living? Everything is getting ultra-personalized. So how does this effect product design and building design? The industry for security on buildings is certainly booming.

In one position of employment, I didn't meet my colleagues for seven months because of the local lockdowns. Further ahead, you could be in a job where you never personally meet many of your immediate colleagues, yet collaborate on projects for a number of years, because you do not need to meet. Plenty of projects are executed between various company offices around the world whilst those involved might never actually meet.

Can a company operate without an office? How do they communicate their brand and style? Previously you stopped 'representing' the company when you walked out of the door at 6pm (more like 11pm when there's a deadline approaching). But now you are representing the company whilst you sit at home, with friends and family in the background. If the company doesn't physically 'exist', but you represent it all the time, you represent it in your house on the screen and therefore that projects a certain image of the company. Where does your business life and private life divide? It used to be at the front door of the building, but not now.

Digitisation

During my upbringing, the power of the internet was just being realized. The world's biggest companies were plotting the future as it is now, in the 1980s and 1990s. I remember hearing about the most incredible and to be honest ludicrous idea that for example, Google would effectively photograph nearly every street in the world. It seemed crazy. But now, you could walk yourself down nearly any street on earth, right now, in pretty good photographic quality, on your mobile phone or computer screen. That undertaking seemed absolutely laughable, but here we are with that option. Taking that 'evolution' a step further, I think travel will merge with 'experiences', the result being that you won't need to go round the world to visit somewhere that interests you. It will be easier to get the headset on, have a version of street view plugged in to the screen view, with the aid of tiny cameras set up in the streets, so that you can connect between your actual location, and be somewhere else entirely. Does this mean potentially less people travel for tourism because you can have such a realistic version of a place, via virtual reality?

Getting really strange now, but there will have to be a version of the whole world, online. It is already partly there. Like a combination of Google street view and all the digital twin models or 'Sketch-Up' projects that are generated and loaded onto Google earth's 3D view. I can definitely see a future where your last project model would be integrated into this online world, combining with all the other projects that architects have completed. So if you have the headset on, you could virtually walk around anywhere in the world, with the real view being shown or sometimes being replaced by a model. The possibilities are truly endless and, in my opinion, and hugely dangerous too. If camera touchpoints are set up to give you a real time experience, then you really are in two places at once. Proving where your 'real self' was at a particular time in the sense of crime solving could be very interesting. You've probably seen some of the brilliant pre-crime films that paint this sort of picture, so again the superb film maker minds have shaped what we might be exposed to.

I think the digital world will allow for changes to be made to its digital version. A completed building in real life still functions that way it is, but when you put on the headset to visit another virtual location for a visit or meetings, maybe those faults within the building will be corrected or over-written once you enter in with a headset on. You are midway between a fake world and a real one. The surfaces, finishes, effects, and locations could be vastly different because they have been amended. What amazing repercussions that has. Who is going to keep updating this online world? Who has responsibility for it? You will be able to find incredible versions of all the world's famous buildings that have been modeled online, but is it the real version? The digital world has no ends and it's kind of frightening.

Architecture in 30 years

Personalisation

So back to design matters, and beyond 2050, buildings

will continue to be an integral part of our lives, but they might be controlling us more. Performing tasks, supplying energy, and being adaptable. The idea of displaying personalised messages dependent on when we walk past and connect via bio recognition, has been floated as a reality for a few years. I think buildings will move and react to climate conditions, capturing resources and sharing them locally as necessary. I think buildings will have moving parts based on occupant's preferences or owner choice, orienting to the sun or being temporarily branded in certain ways, like a further development of screens and LED all over buildings today, giving us information about our health or daily schedule.

Could small modular buildings move elsewhere in the world at will? For a competition entry at an architects practice I worked in, I designed a pod-living scheme, directed at those who want to live in ultra-flexible freedom. The idea was moving house to different places on a week to week basis, also suiting the remote working trend. The upwardly mobile single apartment living was my target sector. This project proposed a network or grid system structure, much like a 3D abacus set up, where each square volume of space, or 'pod', can plug into this connected lattice of structural branches, which incorporate pipework, ductwork, services and cables, with flexibility and movability at the push of a button. Because of each pod's size, you could relocate fairly easily either by simple truck 'removal' of your pod, or probably drone technology. Every movement is of course tracked so you can be accurately billed and traced. Young, single people often like the changeability of life, wanting to move around more, they don't have so many possessions, and can adapt to various environments. A living space of around 9 cubic meters wouldn't seem comfortable, but for ultra-cheap rent and ultimate flexibility, I think something along these lines will eventuate.

Travel

I wasn't alive at the time, but 50 years ago, travel must have been an even more amazing and quite exclusive experience. You could only really research other cultures in books, or savour the stories and experiences from someone else who went there. About 25 years ago travel had become an incredibly common and popular part of life. Only a few years from now, after the huge upsurge in technology advancement for video calls, companies operating fully by screen technology would make it almost unnecessary to travel. A 20km journey into the Melbourne CBD seems slightly wasteful now, let alone the day flights and overnight company trips. For business trips, employees were spending more time in transit than actually attending useful meetings with colleagues. Better and better representations of ourselves on screen is likely, and surely including holograms soon, so that human interaction by screen or face to face is nearly identical.

Two very futuristic options for our further and relentless development of the earth are mega-high living and underwater life. Again, I look to the past on these things to inform the future. 100 years ago, building technology had innovated enough to construct quite high towers. But they have just got taller and taller every decade since. Is there a realistic limit beyond our current height of nearly 1km high? Similarly underwater, all it takes is an extended version of what we already do in terms of scuba diving, air pressure understanding, retaining walls, ultra-strong glass and the storage of oxygen. These ideas are only limited by human wishes. It seems whatever we want to do with our lives, if there is a will to live somewhere, and a fee available to design it, we will find a way.

For some really extreme ideas, give 5 minutes research to 'Alantropa', 'Hyperloop' (not far away from a reality), 'Biosphere 2', geoengineering, and the 'NASA Journey to Mars'. All fascinating projects that are changing the buildings we live in and what we can achieve each day. They all need to be designed.

2.7 ARCHITECTURAL GLOSSARY

I wanted to include a glossary of architectural terms in this book, despite it only being realistic to include a small percentage of the terms you might encounter. It is not a full architectural dictionary, and I will not bother with the easy ones, but the following are some terms that particularly stick out that I was confused by, or needed some specific research to fully understand their application. There are occasionally different interpretations, and it's always advisable to check out some diagrams so you can visualise, but it's a good start.

Needless to say, the power of a Google search should be frequently used. You should adopt a mindset of being inquisitive whenever you don't know a term, so that you solve the knowledge gap straight away. You could say there's nearly 1000 architectural terms to learn (as a very generic estimation), and you might currently be on about 80 to 100 by now, so each one you tick off improves your knowledge. A particular favourite resource of mine is designingbuildingswiki.

Architect - Wikipedia says this is someone who plans, designs and oversees the construction of buildings. The 'chief builder'.

Arcade - is an external but covered corridor or walkway, usually with columns or posts to the open side of the corridor, and the solid wall of a building to the other side. The open side could also have arches and vaults. Typically used in courtyards or alongside an elevation of a building. A classic example being around St Mark's Sqaure in Venice.

Architrave - (or molding) is the 'edging' pieces around an architectural feature, mostly commonly the thin covering trim around doors. Its purpose looks decorative, but functionally it covers up the joint between the plasterboard wall and timber door frame. Check out 'architrave detail' diagrams online.

Arris - this is a way of finishing the edge details of a material or object, with a diagonal angled shape. Often specified on door panel edges, glass edges, or stone edges, but can be a little bit misinterpreted in my experience with all the other edge shapes you can create. Take a look online.

Atrium - in modern day buildings, it's usually a hugely volume of internal, glazed entrance space, several storeys high and often an entrance lobby. It's usually very light and forms a kind of interior conservatory. Very common in hotels or museums.

Aggregate - part of the ingredients for making concrete. Aggregates are the slightly larger stones/rocks in the mix. A huge variety of aggregates, additives, and ingredients can go into concrete mixes to create various strengths, colours, quality characteristics or effects.

Air space / cavity – traditionally brick walls were made from an inner layer (or leaf) and an outer layer, hence making an air gap or 'cavity' between them. Fundamentally it's intended to trap air in this cavity, to keep the inner leaf warmer than the outer leaf. The next step is to attach insulation to the inner leaf (hence still inside the cavity) to keep it warmer still. You can have a cavity space in nearly any wall construction, but most commonly found in external walls or glass units too.

Allowance(s) / Provisional Sum - an amount of money set aside in the construction contract for items which have not been selected and specified yet. For example, selection of flooring tiles may require an allowance instead of knowing the cost immediately. To use a daily example, if you're trying to estimate your weekly food shopping cost, but you don't know the cost of fresh fruits, you can give a 'provisional sum' of 10$ just to give an approximate cost to be reserved.

Contingency – a contingency sum is used as a bit of extra money, reserved for when and if things go wrong on the project. All projects (should) have contingency, so that if things take longer or are slightly more expensive, then there was some 'contingency' money set aside to cover it.

Anchor bolts - structural heavy-duty fixings, to fix or hold something down in place, often where steel columns or posts would be fixed to concrete floors, using the steel plate footing.

Apron – it's not seen that often, but just below a window sill there may be a flat panel or apron, which acts like a skirt in a way, as a decorative and protection board. It deflects rain away from the walls and joints (which are the weak points of any building).

Baluster - a vertical element that effectively forms part of a balustrade or alongside the stairs. Often timber or stone, they help to ensure people wouldn't fall through or under the handrail of stairs.

Bargeboard - when a roof overhangs an external wall, bargeboards are the facing panels to effectively close-off and protect the build-up of the roof, again fundamentally water protection, so pretty similar to aprons above.

Battens – multipurpose pieces of wood, usually square or rectangular, used as a gridded or lattice framework for fixing onto, which also allows air flow because of their depth. Battens are very common in wall lining applications and roofing tiles application. Best to look this up for a quick diagram or picture.

Barrel vault - it's an elongated archway, like an extruded arch, hence forming a kind of semicircular roofed corridor.

Bay window - quite a domestic feature and often on the ground floor, it's a window that has been built as a box that projects or hangs out from the building, sometimes it allows you to have a bench on the inside to sit in.

Bond - in terms of laying bricks into patterns, the way they arranged is called the type of bond. Instead of just stacking them on top of each other, overlapping gives more strength and a better aesthetic appearance. There are lots of bond types to check out if you are that interested.

Bracket - a very loose term for generic small metal clips or angles of all kinds. There's all manner of brackets, just like the type found at standard hardware or DIY stores.

Box gutter - self-explanatory when you think about it, but intended for large volumes of water flow, often between two down-sloping roofs. Massive roofs like airports or warehouses have to deal with huge volumes of water drainage, so the gutters need to be carefully calculated and pretty major details.

Brise soleil - a French term, for some reason adopted quite universally, they are shading devices attached to exterior walls to protect inhabitants from direct sunlight. Could also be called shading fins or blades.

BIM Management Plan (BMP) - there will be a ton of BIM acronyms for you to learn, about executing projects according to certain rules or agreements, but this general one is a plan to outline roles and responsibilities of the project team.

Building Management System (BMS) - a term used to describe the daily operation system of a building, like an instruction manual for how to use it, like the control room, HVAC, security cameras, motion sensors, electronics, cooling, etc.

BIM Coordinator / Manager— this is a recently developed role in the industry, basically to keep all the modelling and BIM integration running smoothly within a business. Responsible for establishing and applying day to day standards and protocols so the team work collaboratively and efficiently share information.

BMS (BMS) building maintenance system — not to be confused with the above, all buildings need cleaning. At low level this is done usually with giant hoses and long handled brushes, but for large buildings there will be huge roof-based cranes that hold a 'cleaning cradle' or allow cleaners to abseil down the façade to wash it. On large buildings this is a serious piece of design. Take a look on Google earth to see roof layouts for the cleaning cradles or boom arms.

Brick course — each layer of brick is called a course; hence you can have various arrangements, sometimes projecting slightly to create patterns.

Backfill - when you dig out a space for the basement below ground level, build the basement walls, then pile all that earth back in against the outside of the wall (with specialist insulation and waterproofing first), that's called backfilling.

Backing / pattress — an internal strengthening frame, usually timber, installed inside the wall to give a strengthened fixing location for heavier accessories like toilets, cabinets, towel bars or grab rails. This is because the regular plasterboard wall won't have enough strength for the fixings to hold them.

Ballast - basically its pebbles and stones providing stability, often used on roof. It covers up ugly surface layers, but still allows drainage through to the outlets. It also stops leaves or debris potentially blocking it.

Batt – insulation comes in batts or rolls, and there are plenty of standard sizes to fit in between standardised wall studs. Often about 600mm wide, around 80mm thick, but lots of variations exist.

Load Bearing wall - a wall that holds vertical load directly above it, hence an important perimeter or structural wall.

Bifold door - just take one regular swinging door leaf, but cut the leaf down the middle and add hinges, so the door folds in on itself.

Bottom and top chord – the horizontal members of a structural truss, similar in arrangement to the web and flange of steel I beams. Find a diagram.

Brick lintel - a strong metal 'L' shaped support angle (kind of a shelf) that bricks sit on, in order to make the window, door opening. There's a whole world of brick detailing and accessories to learn about

Brick tie or wall tie - crucial for brick wall rigidity, these are metal strips laid horizontally into the mortar joint of the inside face of the wall leaves. All part of the brick walls subject.

Butt hinge- the standard hinge type, but there are so many. One piece attaches to the door's edge, the other to the jamb.

CAD Computer Aided Design - Pretty old school now, but the overall name for CAD.

Casework, Cabinetry, joinery items – all quite generic, loosely-used terms, encompassing furniture, internal cupboards, worktops, cabinets, maybe shelving, built in wardrobes, benches etc. Typically made from timber boards, frames, battens and the woodwork.

CFD Computational Fluid Dynamics - very impressive modern software to analyse airflows, ventilation, fire and smoke movement, and typical behaviour models of building occupants, etc. Therefore, this is crucial at design stage and for consultants of that specialism.

Cantilever - where the structural genius happens, cantilevers create suspended overhangs from material strength and engineering magic, but all based on solid mathematics and physics.

Capital - the tops of columns often have a decorative or themed capital, usually more found in historical, political or official buildings.

Casement window - you could call this the standard window, hinged on the side, swinging inward or outward. Generally, the height is greater than the width.

Clerestory - these are usually high windows, often way above eye height, intended as a design feature and to get light deep into rooms.

Classification systems — think of a shopping supermarket analogy, every product is strictly arranged, ordered and located: frozen items, tins, fresh fruit, cereals, bread, lentils. Buildings need that level of organization too for tracking and listing building elements, but there are several classification databases in operation. Classification and data management is crucial in projects.

Coping (or capping) - if a wall projects up beyond the level of the roof, that creates a parapet. On top of this parapet is a capping or coping, for waterproofing reasons and giving a neat finish to wrap over the top of the wall construction. It's usually a folded metal sheet, but could be stone. Worth a quick Google.

Cornice - decorative horizontal feature that forms a small projecting edge from a beam that joins the top of columns

Caulking - used to seal a gap or fill a joint with mastic for waterproofing and prevent leaks.

Chase – it's an untidy but deliberate way of chipping away a channel in a wall (or floor) to allow pipes / cables / wiring to sit snugly into this groove. It's easier to cut this channel after concrete is built, than trying to form it whilst pouring concrete.

Collar joint - a sleeve joint device usually for sealing around a vent. It's helpful for waterproofing, acting in the same way as a collar around your neck.

Control joint - a deliberate joint in concrete, or layout of tiles, where the building can move slightly under the stresses of the weight and materials, so the control joint can absorb that movement.

Door jamb – the surrounding thin boards which a door closes and opens directly onto. Look closely where the door actually rests against the 'door stop' piece. Similar to architraves, but more functional instead of decorative.

Deliverables – the drawings and documents that you have to 'deliver' to the client at various stages of the project, in order to complete that stage, and therefore get paid. Usually set out as a shopping list of requirements, you should find them listed out in the contract documents.

Design + Construct (D&C) or Design + Build (D+B) – a very common method of contract used to execute a project. Where a client has hired one company, therefore one point of contact (and blame / responsibility) to produce a project for an agreed price. All responsibility then falls on that Contractor to get it done, so they design and construct the project.

Plasterboard / Fibreboard / Particleboard – extremely common for interior walls and ceilings. There's a huge number of board variants, fixed onto the stud framing (which can be timber or metal studs). Search the White Book, or Red Book in Australia. It is wall detailing heaven.

Drip molding or drip detail – a tiny but crucial part of rainwater detailing. At an overhanging part of building or detail, or at the top of external walls, water will drip down a surface, pick up dirt or dust and the building will get dirty. But if the overhang has a slight edge detail or indent built in, it will drip off just away from the building face. Look up a quick image of this. Whenever you see bad staining on a building, it's often because of the lack of a good drip detail.

Dormer - there may still be usable space in sloping building roofs, so a horizontally projecting window box allows good use of roof space, and called a dormer window. Very common in domestic houses.

Damp proof course - one of the most fundamental details in design and construction of buildings. This stops water creeping into the exterior materials of the building and transferring through to the interior. It can be plastic waterproof sheeting, or historically a sealant like tar. Definitely look this one up for further understanding about capillary action of water. Good bit of science.

Eaves – as a sloping roof comes down to meet an external wall, if it passes past the line of the wall, that's the eaves. There's lots of roof terminology to look up, best with a diagram.

Expansion joint – much like movement joints or control joints, this allows movement of huge forces on building, like concrete floors or external walls. Typically, the joint will be 30mm or more, with compressible filler between it for elasticity, and this will be way thicker for larger buildings.

Facilities Management - managing and maintaining buildings on a day-to-day basis, consisting of all the building systems, networks, computers, and functions. This is becoming far more important because of the ability to store lots of digital info about buildings, therefore better maintenance, operation, analysis, and control.

Flashing – a crucial part of detailing and waterproofing, flashing is usually a flexible material, often a rubbery felt mat, but can be aluminium or malleable metal. It forms a barrier against any water getting into the details. Flashing is most common in roofing, but also needed for waterproof floor constructions, external walls and then building features where there is any risk that water could enter. A good one to look up and understand it's importance, because it's a crucial part of external detailing.

FF&E Furniture, Fixtures & Equipment - the more you think of it, the more this is a huge scope of work, hence it often needs its own schedule and drawings. The Interior designer often leads this.

Fascia - similar in theory to bargeboard, but this is at the bottom of the sloping part of the roof, and is the visible 'face' panel of the detail.

Fairfaced concrete – often seen in basement areas, like car parks or back of house storage areas, where there is little importance placed on the aesthetic, so the blockwork or concrete surfaces are left 'bare'.

Felt – very common for various applications, but in my experience mostly in roofing, there are many building-felt type products. In general, building felt keeps the water out, but allows air to circulate.

Furring / shim strips - Strips of wood, used to provide minor gradients for surfaces, kind of like a wedge.

Glued Laminated Beam (Glulam)- A structural beam comprised of wood laminations, bonded with adhesives and heated whilst pressured. Extremely strong, and makes a dynamic looking space. Very cool when designed well.

Grade - another word for Ground level.

Grout – it's the coloured final substance that goes in the tile joints, usually in bathrooms or kitchens, to keep water out and fill the gaps perfectly. A similar version of this externally is 'pointing' for brickwork.

Gable - in a pitched roof condition, the wall beneath it is called a gable wall, where in essence is still just a wall. Check out an overall roof diagram for all the roof terms, there really is a lot.

Hip roof - a roof type with all sides sloping the same way.

HVAC – abbreviation for Heating, Ventilation and Air Conditioning. The engineers often have this entire area covered under one Services company scope.

Hardware / ironmongery – for several years I never quite understood the term ironmongery, but it's all the accessories on doors, windows or fixings, like door knobs, door handles, locks, kick plates, door closers, and often represented in a long hardware schedule for exactly which door or accessory it belongs to.

Infiltration - The natural passage of air or water in and out of buildings; usually associated with cracks, seams or holes in buildings. It's a strange dichotomy to think that an absolutely air tight building or room wouldn't get any fresh oxygen in, so when building design attempts to be air tight, it's kind of saying that the details and joints will be perfectly air tight even though you would actually need some air infiltration into the building. PassivHaus is a good subject to do 10 mins research about.

Insulating Glass – a big innovation area for energy saving, the standard double glazed was always two leaves of glass with air between, then the inner pane can be laminated for extra safety and insulation. Argon gas was used to fill the cavity, but now krypton makes even better insulation, although expensive. Triple glazed glass is becoming more common, but very expensive. Worth 10 minutes research on: double glazed units DGUs, Low-Emissivity, Low Iron, laminated glass.

IFC (Industry Foundation Classes) - IFC is an open, global data model file, designed for the BIM era data exchange.

Joist – is a horizontal beam in a floor or roof, usually structural. It allows room between each joist for cabling or air circulation. Usually timber or steel.

Compression and tension – structural elements are under tension or compression, depending on the forces above it pushing down, or the forces of various elements all acting on each other to create amazing spans and shapes. Look up some diagrams about simple roof structure stresses.

Lintel - usually spanning across a door or window head, this horizontal beam (concrete or timber usually) allows safe construction of the structural opening, and therefore the loading above the door or window.

Lead consultant – a term to describe the company employed to lead the design of a project, usually the architect. They have control over the other building consultants i.e., structural engineer, mechanical electrical plumbing (MEP), or landscape. The traditional arrangement is for clients to use the architects as their design lead.

Level of Development (LOD) - more BIM terminology, to decide how detailed your model and output info will be. Ranging from 100 to 500. Good to look up a quick guide, as some clients use it a lot, other people will tell you it's more trouble than it's worth.

Laminating – process of bonding together two or more layers of materials. Very important in glazing, but plenty of building materials get extra strength by laminating, such a cross laminated timber. Think of when a piece of paper gets laminated, in essence it just has an extra layer stuck to it, for a bit more rigidity.

Lath - a device to allow application and good adhesion of plaster, good for corners, or attachments of tiles, can be wood, metal, and very common in construction circles, probably on sale at your local DIY store.

Louvre – louvres can be applied to wall panels, doors or windows. They are usually horizontal but can sometimes be vertical, they are parallel, closely aligned, angled blades (typically about 30 to 40 degrees from the vertical plane) that visually screen unsightly items, but allow ventilation into a space, hence commonly used in mechanical plant rooms.

Masonry – a generic term for stone, brick, concrete, blocks, or other similar building units or materials.

Mastic - A handy sealing material and a term that is very generically used for pushing glue-like paste into cracks and forming a neat waterproof seal. The simplest usage example is at the corner of the bath to seal it to the wall, but mastic seal is used all over buildings, particularly cladding details.

Miter joint- if two pieces are joining at 90 degrees angle, a mitred joint means a diagonal cut to make the end of each piece 45 degrees each.

Mansard roof - often containing livable roof space, it's a roof with a steep face which then transitions into a shallower gradient to the top. Thus, a two-part roof.

Mechanical, Electrical, Plumbing (M+E or sometimes MEP) – the engineering scope of work is often lumped together, known as a Services company, because it's better to have one company coordinating all those disciplines together.

Mortar – sand, lime and cement, mixed and use on brick joints, it eventually seals and hardens to be waterproof and protective to the surface. If you ever get a chance to see a bricklayer at work for a few minutes, watch carefully.

Molding - a general decorative term for finishing door panels and edging in timber

Mullion - the central vertical element in a window separating two pieces of glass. Generally, transoms are horizontal, mullions are vertical.

Over panel – are used when a door has a glass panel directly above it, usually just for getting natural light into the entrance hall without having a see-through door pane.

Parapet - when an external wall connects to the roof, the external wall might continue up above the roof level, which therefore forms a parapet wall, which then needs a capping or coping.

Pelmet - usually an interior application, it's a panel or covering, intended to cover or hide the top of curtains or blinds. It's a pretty old-fashioned domestic detail in my experience.

Pilaster - a column that has been embedded in a wall, thus slightly projecting, but not always a structural element.

Particle board - used in all manner of ways all over jobs, but particle board is sawdust all compressed and glued with resin. Often in roofing, floorboards, or sometimes casing for joinery items, furniture or shelving etc.

Partition – most basically, it's a wall that subdivides spaces. Internal partitions are commonly just plasterboard panels fixed to metal or timber studwork.

Party wall – I first thought this was a shortened name for 'Partitions', but it's slightly different. It separates 2 properties, which gets very messy when an owner on one side of the wall is trying to execute some construction work.

Paver, paving stones - sometimes called flags or slabs for external application.

Pitch line – often for dimensioning stair handrails, so in section view of a stair, if you were to draw a straight line which touches the edge of each stair, that's the pitch line, and therefore the gradient.

Plenum – I heard this term a lot in early years, and often incorrectly, but the air supply and extract go through the plenum, in terms of HVAC systems. Check out ductwork and ceiling void arrangements.

Plumb – if something is described as plumb, it's exactly vertical and perpendicular to the flat ground.

Plywood - wood board made of layers of timber, compressed, glued and joined under huge pressure. Can be very strong for boarding, in roofs or floors much like particle boards.

Point load - A point where a bearing / structural weight is concentrated and transferred to the foundation. Think of a standard kitchen table, the overall weight of the object is slightly different to the exact pressure point of each leg pushing on the floor.

Post-and-beam goalpost- as it suggests an extremely simple structure like a football / soccer goalpost.

PVC or CPVC - Poly Vinyl Chloride – it's worth a few minutes getting your head around the standard functions of plastics i.e., guttering is often PVC, supermarket plaster bags are polyethylene. Polypropylene is often for pipes or rigid plastic.

Porte-cochère - translates to a canopy in standard English, and often seen at hotels as a grand entrance experience, it's a shelter effectively, just a projecting roof for cover from the weather.

Pointing – the final protection layer of applying mortar to external joints, the pointing layer is the neat final finish surface, still waterproof and protective like mortar, but often coloured to suit the wall appearance.

Practical completion – a crucial contractual term, but as it sounds, the building is practically complete. This is an official stage where all parties agree, but just a few small items are still outstanding to be cleaned up and finished off. It's a very crucial part of signing off a project for all parties.

Return detail – slightly difficult to explain, but often described as the edge or face around the corner from the item you're talking about, when the material 'returns' at an angle to meet the building. The return details 'closes off' the material.

Rafter – the large sloping structural element in a roof laid parallel usually.

Request for Information (RFI) - a phrase which is hugely useful in coordination tasks. Instead of having thousands of emails asking questions, it's very useful to record all questions and answers about any discrepancies. The chart usually shows: date, raised by, what issue, attachment, of a design solution sketch, when to answer by, and resolution.

Rebar / reinforcing bar – structurally talking, the concrete being poured into place needs to bind onto something, hence steel is used to knit it together. Look up a diagram or site picture for this. It's like a skeleton concealed into the concrete mass. And whilst you're there give 5 minutes to pouring concrete and formwork. Loads to learn.

Retaining wall - A structural wall that holds back earth on a slope and prevents erosion. Retaining walls are crucial for basement and below ground level construction, because of the pressure of all that earth pushing against it.

Stair Riser / stair tread - vertical distance from one stair level to the next. Regulations govern how much this can be in buildings, usually around 180mm. The tread is where your foot lands.

Rough opening or structural opening – commonly used term giving the dimensions of a window or door opening, before the actual item is installed, to ensure the item can fit into the structural opening. Eg, if a door was 940mm wide, the structural opening might be about 1020mm, to give 30mm packing, sealing and tolerance for each side.

Stair Nosing - for edge protection and often incorporating slip resistance, L shaped profiles fit over the front edge of the step, with many inserts for grip and visual differentiation. Have a quick search for examples.

Screed – used in various floor construction, poured on top of a concrete slab, screed is a thin layer anything from 25mm – 150mm thick, to provide a kind of bedding for the final finish to come in. Screeds can form the final finish, but need sealant and binding. Look up a quick detail.

Shim - much like packing, scrap timber can be used to

pack out gaps and allow minute little adjustments if something is just a few millimeters away from being solidly packed in.

Soffit - most basically the underside cladding of a covered area or over-hanging roof.

Specifications or Specs - almost like the instruction manual of projects. In project documentation, broadly the drawings show where, the schedules show what, and the specs show how. Specs are written with extreme detail and clarity, so the builder will know exactly what is needed to make the installation, and what materials and accessories to use.

Stringer – the side panel of a stair. The ends of the stair treads piece fit into the stringer.

Stud - A vertical wood or metal framing member used in simple wall construction, attached top and bottom to give the wall its rigidity and strength.

Suspended ceiling - if you were to take off the finish layer of a ceiling above you, most likely there is a gap from that surface to the structural floor slab above. That space is the ceiling void, and the system to build that is often suspended with rods and metal ties in order to use that ceiling space for ductwork, cables and lighting units.

Snagging – at the end of a project, the architect will compile a list of many very small items that are not crucial to the operation of the building as a whole, but need to be corrected or repaired before official completion. Often just small marks and minor repairs to make, they are quite superficial but important to ensure the final bit of quality.

Spandrel - like a covering panel, often this obscuring panel is located at floor level to block out the slab edge behind, common in panels of glass wall or cladding. Can be a big part of the façade design.

Sarking – like a waterproof layer that's underneath the visible surface, acting as a second barrier when water gets in, comes in large sheets so the fixing of them is crucial.

Threshold – the exact point transitioning from one room into the other, where two floor surfaces join. A threshold strip, commonly metal, is often used to cover the joint.

Transom - window elements which are horizontal, mullions are the vertical, transoms are the horizontal.

Taped joints - when plasterboards abut each other to form a flat wall or ceiling, they can be taped at the joint to form a clean connection, ready for painting or finishing.

Tolerance – buildings are dealing with massive elements and forces and therefore plenty of movement, thus you commonly hear that 'tolerance' is built-in to the detailing, to accept that things might be a few millimeters out. Typically, concrete walls or floors will be made within 15-25mm plus or minus tolerance, other things should be a bit more accurate but not absolutely exact.

Vapor barriers and membranes - installed on exterior walls and ceilings to restrict movement of water vapor into walls and prevent condensation within them. Normally, polyethylene plastic sheeting is used. Should be installed in such a way to reduce any risk of being pricked or damaged.

Veneer - Extremely thin sheets of wood applied to cheaper wood, to make something look better. Used on furniture as a finish for pattern purposes. Hence the veneer layer can give a prime looking finish.

Ventilation shaft - there are many shafts in tall buildings, taking a variety of pipes, ducts, cables, air, waste chutes and of course lifts up and down a building. Some small ones are just for ventilation. Check out a standard core plan for a large building, to see where all the shafts are fitted in.

Variation Order (VO) - hugely important and inevitable part of understanding projects, if a design needs to change slightly, but will affect the cost. This needs to be tracked and recorded before the cost or impact gets out of hand. If building your own house for example, you'd want to know if the main contractor was going to change materials designs which would affect the over cost. Much to read about on this one.

Weatherstrip - Narrow sections of material (like foam) can be installed to prevent the infiltration of air and moisture around windows and doors edges. Can be brushes or flaps, or a compressible pad. Very important addition for external doors and windows.

Wayfinding – signs for finding your way around a building, but more directionally orientated. There are lots of types of signage, which might be split up in your project.

Weep holes – found on bricks or on the horizontal part of window frames, they allow drainage of water, just in case a build-up of water or condensation occurs. Also allows a tiny amount of airflow. Hence the absolute air tight design process becomes slightly flawed. Worth a 5mins research.

Ziggurat - basically a pyramid with stepping levels as opposed to a flat slope.

As ever, if in doubt, have a further look at definitions from other sources yourself, because there are so many avenues for answers these days, often conflicting each other.

SECTION 3 - AUTOBIOGRAPHY

I'm glad you have made it this far, and have hopefully learnt a few things by now. This section of the book is purely the story of my career experiences.

As mentioned, I graduated in 2005 and have been in architectural employment pretty much every year since then, so the final part of this book charts that story, with all the exciting, painful, funny or demoralising experiences, exactly as they happened. I think it is important that you remember or record all the experiences you have, as they happen. Good and bad are both valuable.

3.1 UPBRINGING

- Hometown
- Design is a solution
- Analysing
- Teach yourself

Hometown

An architecture career was really not on the radar in my schooling years, so don't worry if you are a complete beginner. Academically, I was at a proficient level across the board, without specializing in any subject. Maths, English, Science and Geography came fairly easily, whilst I had a bit more flair for Design Technology, but no absolute stand-out talent. I was able to put my mind to a subject and satisfy the necessary requirements, without exactly innovating or deep thinking. I think the secret to school exams (aged 16 years in UK) and A-Level exams (aged 18 years) was to study something and basically regurgitate it in a different way to show your understanding. How do you best show your aptitude and how can you most easily tick the boxes? Not to sound lazy, but in some ways, what is the quickest and easiest way to success, whilst still doing a thorough job. I think architecture is an artistic and intellectual subject where more effort should result in better output. It is not a subject to short cut, and it is always important to remember the simplicity of what architecture really is.

My first chance to seriously 'design' something was in Design and Technology for my A level exams. The various tasks were to design a modern looking kettle, then a child's toy, then what really piqued my interest was a new football stadium for my hometown in the UK. I was learning why my hometown was architecturally unusual, and starting to understand why and how it is different from other towns. This level of analysis and critique was a good grounding. Similarly to the products I had designed, I was understanding that design has to serve a purpose. It needs to give a solution to a problem.

Design is a solution

All around us are very simple objects that need very simple designs for a very simple function. I wondered how such massive powerful industries, like product design or the automotive industry, could still have room for improvement. How can we not be at the optimum standard of design by now? How can you possibly design a fork incorrectly? Or a plate? Or a kettle? Seeing how many design interpretations are on the market, requiring millions of pounds of investment or thousands of hours work, showed what huge variety there is in design, and therefore demand. There is such a wide spectrum of architectural design, because there is such a wide spectrum of personal interpretation.

Do customers change their preferences for designers to react to, or do the designers produce solutions to convince the customer what they need? My realization was that the world develops and changes according to people's needs and wants. Does design respond to a change, or make the change itself? It is human nature to like objects, things, belongings, and products. We seem to value new things that function a little better than before, or with better options, or if they look better. Cost and convenience are usually the most influential, but it is good to realise and understand that the world depends on design progress too. Improving the quality of products, facilities, or services that you use, gradually improves your quality of life.

Analysing

My hometown, Milton Keynes in the middle of the UK, is arranged on a grid pattern of roads, making square housing clusters between them. Having read plenty of books about its design approach and origins, and comparing against the fundamental ideals of this planned town, I realised the theory generally did work. But the theory was based on the assumption that residents want their town to be ruled by and shaped by the use of a car. When Milton Keynes was being planned in the 1960s, this wasn't a bad concept. Travelling quickly on the faster 'grid' roads ensured slower driving in the estates where people lived. However, after 25 years of the city being created, the city does not function well because the world changed so rapidly in terms of transport and use of time. The design quickly became outdated by what people do with their lives, and large areas of the town became very empty and too bland.

It is an interesting place to grow up, not that I knew it at the time. It was a good lesson to revisit several years after my architectural education, and understand how to improve the failings. The vast boulevards and bare concrete ended up looking quite stale, and especially after around 7pm, many central locations were not populated hence the visual result was a concrete wasteland. Many buildings had no design personality and were very exposed in their context. The city looked very modern, and tidy, and deliberate, but it lacked soul and a bit of love. Densities are crucial for creating livable and vibrant places, but especially in the town center, it did not really work because everything was so rigidly spaced out.

Milton Keynes does not feature in many historical or theoretical architecture books, but for some reason it gives me hours of interest, study and analysis. Quite a lot of my thoughts are 'what could have been' but that's a very easy way to view it. Examples of similarly interesting architectural and planning strategies are present in Canberra in Australia, Los Angeles in USA, or Brasilia in Brazil. In Milton Keynes, (and perhaps you could say anywhere), the people of the town are the ultimate 'customers.' They define its success. Inhabitants should appreciate and understand the reasons for the planning and architectural style. I would really recommend ten minutes of your time having a quick Google Earth tour and researching the layout of the town.

In the center of Milton Keynes particularly, the building typologies were clear. Materials were modern, clean and safe, but looked quite basic. You cannot really locate yourself easily as a visitor, because large areas of the town look very similar, especially from the road network. There are a few buildings I look back on now with such familiarity and fondness, not because I loved the architecture, but because they are memorable places of childhood activities. In a reverse kind of way, the architecture was having a lasting effect on me, despite being quite negative. I think you can analyse architecture from an angle of memories and association. People don't love London because they have visited all of it. They love it because various locations in the city represent a variety of feelings, depending on their activities, experiences and memories. It's that subconscious relationship with a place or its buildings that I think is important.

Teach yourself

You can critique your own architectural perceptions and opinions, to analyze why you do or do not like various places. Was it the feeling of individual familiarity with a place, or can you accurately explain why you like the built environment? Wherever you grew up, large city or small village, there will always be examples of architecture nearby. It might be basic, it might be boring, it might not inspire much comment or passing thought. But what I learnt from my hometown is to understand and teach yourself why buildings are bad, ugly, and unsuccessful.

3.2 UNIVERSITY

- A choice
- Study harder

- Failure
- Relief

A choice

University seemed to be a natural choice, but a default next step after my A levels. I was not sure what my career path would be or where I would end up. I was lacking life experience. Many people have no idea what they will end up doing when they leave university, let alone the rest of their career. I think it is better to remain open in your intended path. There is a wide variety of professions in the world now, let alone the architecture industry, so you will gradually find your direction. To have a rigid career planned out might be more restrictive and unsettling if it takes a turn in the first few years, because you don't want to be too reliant on just one option.

Architecture qualifications are not just for now. They are more like a step forward on the long journey of life and professional career, allowing you to progress to the next step and improve. It is possible, but difficult, to jump any steps on this life ladder. You generally have to take one step which leads onto the next. After a few years as a postgraduate, your attentions might soon change to the next qualification, or different industry altogether. I was just going to university for the life experience, not really knowing what lay on the other side.

It was quite a stab in the dark for me to choose architecture, but after visiting a few universities and seeing what amazing campuses were available, I just chose what seemed most comfortable. My surroundings were vitally important to being happy and so that was the prime consideration for tackling the challenge ahead. It can feel like the biggest decision of your life, but success in the industry will still be solely down to you, once you have a job, and not necessarily the quality or location of your degree.

During the summer leading up to my acceptance into the Architecture Part 1 course, I did not really discuss, think about or study architecture at all. I couldn't and didn't appreciate the art and skill of design at all. I was not aware enough or perhaps perceptive enough to dive into the history of architecture and find some meaning in the subject. Philosophy, arts, classics, and politics would have been especially useful here as a grounding, although I am not saying it is critical to know these in any sort of depth. Just picking up a few books and getting into the industry would have helped me prepare. With the amount of information so readily available now, it is absolutely crazy not to be inquisitive and dive into the subject, to avoid feeling like a total novice.

Study harder

Year 1 of university was a trap for me. I was not very critical of myself, and was too concerned with enjoying the lifestyle of a protected hub. I made some lifelong friends and do not regret it, but even to open a textbook for a few hours as recommended in lectures, would have been useful. I was beginning a career in architecture, one of the most respected, intelligent, and pure subjects you can find, but I did not take it particularly seriously. I did not engage in any critical thinking, and did not undertake enough historical analysis even with Nottingham's local architecture on my doorstep. I was still lacking the bare bones of construction knowledge and a design eye.

I should have spent more time learning the software too. It was only basic CAD at that point, and I did not learn any Sketch-Up or 3D modelling. In year 2, the main architectural design project was to design a housing scheme on a disused field in a small town in the middle of the UK. My design proposal was for serene looking, low impact 'A'-framed lodges, partly submerged in the ground, in a reversed living arrangement, with living space upstairs and bedrooms underground. It was a nice idea, but poorly executed. I didn't introduce much architectural thought or feeling to the design. The concept was average, but my presentation and drawing skills needed a big improvement. Other students were producing stunning software images or advanced conceptual theories, and I should have produced something attention grabbing and interesting. The next project was a bookshop café brief in a tight city location. The clarity of my drawings was better and communicating my main design ideas became a key point, not just churning out the expected plan, section and elevation. Another short project was a health center in an untidy part of town. My proposal was a gentle, slightly simple but harmonious design, with a greenhouse style courtyard, trying to heighten the emotions and psychology of visiting a health center. But again, my designs became a bit too rigid. I had not created a concept or shown off any personality in the design. My drawings were described as 'naive.' They were too! Perhaps the final straw was a school project, featuring a huge shared courtyard and curved corridors which ended up a bit of a maze. I had a stronger concept overall, but did not produce enough work to communicate it, and had certainly confused myself with distances when it was revealed I had 30-

meter-wide classrooms!

At this point, someone like a mentor to help me sharpen up the presentation side of my projects would have been invaluable. My work looked like an absolute beginner, which I guess I was, but there was not much of an approach towards improvement amongst my tutors, considering this was still year one.

It was invaluable to take a few weeks paid work during the summer, not only to work off some impending debts, but to keep developing skills that were applicable in a day-to-day business environment. I would hugely recommend you to take any work experience whenever you can. You won't be designing buildings every day, but it's all part of learning the industry from the bottom up, so you can appreciate what the whole job entails and therefore have direct knowledge of each level.

I worked on simple steel-framed warehouse buildings in my summer job, using CAD properly for the first time. I was lining up elevations with gridlines, consistently setting out internal walls, and understanding what really goes onto a General Arrangement drawing. I was even taught how to fold A1 sheets correctly, something I am sure very few people need to do now. Sitting in smart work attire in a deadly quiet office, listening to phone calls and surrounding myself with drawings, was a strangely exciting but daunting experience. I did not understand projects then, but my observations were making more sense each day. I remember one colleague was laughing so hysterically on the phone nearly every day, making friends with whoever was on the line. Early lessons still stand true now from that work experience; take the smart approach to listen carefully to others and learn something every day. See how other people do things, learn, and give it a shot yourself. Continual improvement is a massive daily challenge, even in small chunks, but it does not happen by itself and really does not need much effort.

Failure

I think my lack of engagement in year one left me quite exposed to the more brutal year two requirements. I had to re-sit a couple of modules to sufficiently improve. The bad marks pushed me further into my shell psychologically, and certainly left me feeling that I couldn't succeed. I did not really want to admit it to myself, but I needed someone to tell me this is not good enough. I can easily look back now and say I was not putting the number of hours in, to give myself a chance of succeeding. I retook the main design modules in the following year and showed slight improvement, although it was clear that my design and drawing skills were not up to it.

History of Architecture and Construction in Architecture in year two were actually my best module results, probably because I felt there were more right and wrong answers to be guided by. The design crits seemed quite passive and would not really communicate in clear terms how to improve, and my marks were poor. A failing 19/20-year-old architecture student needs a few tips before the design fluency and expression flows. I was too passive, assuming that I would just be spat out at the other end of this degree, equipped for the industry. It was time to confront my failings head on, so I elected to retake some of the main design modules.

I would highly recommend architecture

273

qualifications to allow a year in industry far earlier than is currently done. To understand day-to-day life in practice, and see what is actually important or enjoyable is so pivotal. Far more exposure to the real world would be beneficial. Otherwise sitting there fretting (or sleeping) in lecture halls, staying until the end just to tick the attendance, yet failing to remember a single word of what was actually discussed, is a bad cycle to get into. Even one day a week in a practice where you can produce drawings and be immersed in real projects would have helped me hugely.

It's fair to say year three was a bit of a disaster, with fellow students ramping up their standards to create their amazing looking final submissions. But after average marks in the design modules again, I was given the option to move to the Architecture Studies course. So, I entered a bit of a fresh start in year four. I found the range of modules and theory of the subject much better, coupled with a great dissertation about the social problems of post-war high rise building in the UK. The class sizes were all smaller, therefore it was easier to ask questions and discuss interpretations or opinions. It was a softer environment where you'd actually know everyone's name and chat amongst the lectures, thus appreciating other viewpoints and hearing inquisitive comments.

This course gave me a different approach to architecture, with planning and urban design much more relevant and open, which I really loved. Pure architecture in building form is of course amazing, but none of it would exist without the context in which it is set, and the streetscape overall. Analysing legible cities and why they are successful involved much more critical reading examples and much more engagement from the essay tasks. Compared to working all hours of the day and night on a design that might already be rejected by the examiners, it was a refreshing change.

There was far more exposure to building images in this course, and the time to discuss the 'why' and 'how' of architecture. I learnt lots of building techniques and design styles, and developed a fascination with history of architecture. Within a few weeks I actually found myself looking forward to sitting in the library, reading for several hours about historical or heritage buildings, with explanations and clear reasoning. It is so simple looking back, but to experience a professional summary of why a building is good, why it is right, and why it is good architecture, was a huge help. Sometimes you just need telling what is right, especially in such a subjective topic like architecture.

I was feeling more conviction in my own opinions about architecture and had the willingness to discuss it openly with colleagues. My marks rose into the 70s, and my dissertation just sneaked into a first-class grade. Despite being battered and bruised, I was pretty relieved to come out with a 2:1 and actually had a bit of a spring in my step. I finally had some knowledge to contribute to the world of work.

Relief

Before attempting to find a full-time job, I took some temporary work again. You have got to see the monotonous daily office life sooner or later. Understanding working attitudes, work hours, work attire, business expectations, perhaps even encountering the dreary personalities of some more traditional old school

275

architects, is all important.

It is quite common to have someone in your extended family or network of friends who can connect you with someone in the industry, so that is definitely worth pursuing. Whether that's taking job searching advice, discussing the current industry skills or taking some temporary employment. All those connections will be handy in the future. People you meet when you are young in the industry, are still likely to be there ten or fifteen years later.

For my temporary employment post-graduation, I drew up the elevations on AutoCAD for simple domestic extensions. They were small but important tasks; such as getting the external and internal levels correct around door thresholds, alignment of sills and lintels around the elevations, and correcting labels of title blocks or drawing numbers. I was talking to the technical leads in the office, seeing how they approached work and mostly observing their conversational conduct. I was scared of making phone calls myself, but learnt quickly from how they did it. Their attitude seemed so beneficial to their own development. They were clearly learning something every day. In this role, I saw my two bosses attending relentless meetings and discussing ongoing billing and project costs or deadlines, and always on phone calls. They had a tough business attitude, and hardly seemed to be involved in any design work at all. I realised that each person in the office will have certain specialties, and it won't always be producing drawings.

The work itself was a bit tedious and not very architecturally pleasing. But I saw that some practices have to survive on these projects, the small schemes for a few thousand pounds fee could be the bread and butter. I saw first-hand how tough it is running a business and needing to bring in small sums of money just to keep feeding the staff. It might not give the architectural design freedom you want, but very rarely can you refuse a project opportunity.

The most important lesson of any early work experience or temporary job you find, is to soak up information like a sponge. There generally won't be too much pressure on your output or capabilities initially. A company wouldn't usually rely on a work experience or young staff member to produce critical contract documents. So, use the time effectively whilst there's no pressure. Everything you hear, read or see in the office should be a lesson. After work or at weekends, give yourself enough time to rest and mentally process all the information. During my early jobs, I didn't speak up a great deal, but tried to make lots of notes, remember lots of conversations, and find time to do a little research on the side, so that each day I was slightly better than the last.

Use your work experience time to improve your software skills. Sharpen up your visual and documentation skills that are useful in a professional office, like attention to detail and organisation. There will always be a place in the industry for the person who can make simple 2D and 3D technical drawings, so work experience is a great time to build your real-world skillset.

3.3 FIRST EMPLOYMENT

- ▫ Real world
- ▫ An office
- ▫ My path
- ▫ Resigning

Real world

After the university experience ended in 2005, suddenly it got serious as I began searching for a full-time job. I suppose with temporary employment, you know when the term will end, and often there will not be huge expectations of you. But a paid job, where a company wants consistent high-level output, is entirely different. I wrote simple cover letters to accompany my very basic, bare looking CV, to send via email to various companies in London. At the time, architectural assistants were in high demand, and paying well. A company had replied to my advert answer, and contacted me about the Arsenal Stadium redevelopment that they needed staff for. I was hooked instantly. I had no idea about the company, no idea about the location, and no idea if I was good enough. But they liked my CV, and I was available immediately. It was a case of getting train tickets organised and turn up to give it my best shot. It was clear that my AutoCAD skills were the prime reason to employ me in this role as soon as possible.

An office

The office was pleasant, with a good layout, a big printer room, a staff lounge with tea, coffee and biscuits, and enough space around my desk to pin up some hints and tips I needed on a daily basis. These were things like AutoCAD shortcuts, level colours or naming conventions, measurement conversions or typical details. In my temporary employment I had seen a colleague have lots of notes and reminders pinned up all over his desk wall and computer screen. I could see that continual learning is continual improvement. I bombarded my mind with information at work, so that on the journey home each day, some of it would sink in.

The office structure was not too different from any other 20 to 40-person sized office. The company owner was constantly on the phone or dashing off to meetings, and the project director seemed far too busy to ever chat. There was a project IT and CAD support manager who would answer every question under the sun, several times a day. Then three or four package leaders who worked with the draftsmen or architecture assistants like me. I was certainly in the CAD-monkey group, producing drawings each day for meetings, submissions or to help decide on design decisions. I felt quite important and certainly well needed in the role, although I was just doing what somebody else told me, and doing a job that many other graduates can do. As an architectural assistant, I was basically the last in the chain being instructed which lines to draw where, whilst trying to bring my software skills to the table.

For the first few years in industry, you will be down the bottom of the chain doing what somebody else tells you. That's fine, and normal. Those just above you are still doing what somebody else above tells them, and those at the top are still servicing a client somewhere along the line. Aside from detailing and coordination, my tasks were to discuss design amendments with my equivalents in the consultant teams.

Concerning my first real project, the Arsenal stadium scheme was brilliant. I loved the perfection, precision and visual clarity of using AutoCAD. I began to lead by example by really pushing my understanding of good detailing, being extremely accurate, and questioning how different parts of AutoCAD worked. I asked colleagues how best to do things and often formulated best practice amongst the team after such discussions. I learnt in these months to interrogate drawings very closely. Every line means something, so I needed to be able to identify it, or question it. Drawings can look very complicated and are tough to understand, but they are that way because they need to make perfect sense whilst showing lots of information accurately. I really dived into the role and always seemed to be meeting deadlines with extra time to spare to help others. I soon had a 10% pay rise, as I was digging deeper into my responsibilities and asking how I could get better. It is still the best pay rise I've ever had. I learnt more in 6 months of work than 4 years of university, and made myself a crucial part of the team.

My path

At this stage I had no contractual, management or financial experience of the industry at all. The company wasn't really going to invest time on me learning any of that, so in that sense, it was unnecessary to learn. It is very tough to develop project running knowledge until you are in the thick of that role. Luckily, I had three hours of commute every day to keep learning, so after a hard day's work I would sometimes just think over what the day had brought. I asked lots of questions of colleagues, starting conversations at lunch time, going to seminars or architecture events, and making that real life learning cross over with my social time. A few minutes conversation with someone who you really know and trust, can be much better than trying to plough through online articles or conflicting textbooks.

During my 18 months at the company, I worked almost fully on the windows and cladding package. I knew about all of the aluminium frame details, glazing joints, extrusions, fixings, slab edges, setting out points, glazing surfaces, spacers, gaskets, trims, sills and drainage. This was a period of endlessly searching definitions and ongoing daily design chats with the team. The days seemed to go really quickly being so busy, but researching right to the heart of the issue and being inquisitive was a great habit to keep.

Resigning

As the project slowed down, I was coming to a point where I wanted to move on. The daily travel was becoming a hassle and I had cut my teeth in the stadium job. I got dragged into the basement package in my final two months, coordinating structural walls and parking spaces, whilst also asking the structural engineer to confirm and coordinate the headroom and ramp gradients. It was slightly less enjoyable than windows package but still very valuable to tick off a different part of a building. I saw it as an opportunity to do a job quickly and get past it as soon as possible.

The next new experience was how to hand in my notice. I followed the general online advice of how to write a polite but quick resignation letter. Short, sharp and polite. It was no more than about five sentences, saying I would like to hand in my notice, that I really appreciated working for the company, and finally stating my projected last day at work. It was pretty awkward giving my boss the letter and he wasn't particularly happy. Other people were starting to leave en-masse and this was a good time for a progressive step in my career.

It's good advice not to burn your bridges. However, telling the cold hard truth and backing it up with good reasoning is ok if you really want to communicate some complaints and gripes as you leave a company. No doubt it can sometimes feel good to do so. It is an important skill to be able to speak up and voice constructive criticism. Your manager may recognise your good suggestions and perhaps make some changes. Be genuine, forthright, and thankful that the company gave you the chance to develop your career and grow towards the inevitable next stage.

You have to appreciate that you are a small and fairly cheap part of the team in the early years, and generally you are easily replaced. Your company relies on you doing the right thing for the project and business at that time. The expectation of a 40-year-old architect is quite high, but of a 22-year-old graduate is quite low. Knowing your role and meeting your responsibilities is absolutely number 1 priority. Performing beyond your position and then improving yourself each day is hugely beneficial to any company, but most importantly, crucial for you.

3.4 WORKING IN LONDON

- ▫ Big smoke
- ▫ My niche
- ▫ Diving in
- ▫ Projects
- ▫ Early ambitions

Big smoke

I had registered with a job agency, and they lined up an interview meeting with a company director. I seemed a good prospect for this company. I was 24 years old, had good CAD skills, was very willing to develop and would be committed for several years ahead. In the interview, we went through my limited portfolio, but mostly had a good chat about what I had previously worked on. Most of the discussion just centered around my detailing and coordination. I took smart, clean, tidy drawings at various scales, and diverted discussions towards my maturing technical expertise. The market was buoyant, there were plenty of projects, and I was one of several people joining the company each month.

Straight away I worked on a massive business park scheme near Heathrow airport, with several CAD technicians, around four package leaders, then two project directors, so it was a fairly sizeable team. I had to ask for a lot of CAD help, because this company used MicroStation instead of AutoCAD. It was similar enough in principle, but with different enough commands and buttons to cause problems. It was a bit of a worry at the time, but the company were very patient in helping me learn and knowing my skills would build up.

I enjoyed lunchtime walks or quick museum visits in nearby Westminster, which I saw as all part of developing myself. I wandered round all sorts of streets near the office. I would critique local buildings, chat with work colleagues about their jobs and talk about architecture. I was lucky being in London, with all the cool projects, artistic and inventive schemes, design competitions and exhibitions, with so many opportunities to get involved. It is easy to look back and say it, but you should not coast along in your career for too long. You have to be critical and dedicated with your own development. Take life by the reins, and do everything you can.

My niche

I started to become very competent at MicroStation. Again, I delved deeper into the understanding of it and discovered all the little tricks and shortcuts. I think drawing software is a bit daunting at the start, but once you know the basics, it all works in similar principles. It is not hard to self-teach now, googling everything from using Excel or Word, to Revit commands and shortcuts. Embrace all the little hints that you find. You can potentially elevate yourself above your peers that are less confident or knowledgeable, and become a 'captain' or steering group leader with those skills. It was inevitable for me to join the company CAD group because of those previous six months diving in and wanting to be able to solve problems for others. My increasing awareness of the software basically came from taking tips off the other group members, sometimes making it look like I was the expert around my team. That sort of stuff is loved by your managers. If you are taking initiative and teaching other staff to develop, it is a huge free win for the company.

My typical day was full of creating and amending drawings, to show slight design changes either from my own directors or from consultant's email instructions. I was starting up drawing packages, organising the numbering, and always generating fresh elevations or details to help understand the corner, doorways or ground junctions. During the design phase of the unitized curtain walls, we had a team trip to Dresden in Germany for two nights, assessing and scrutinizing every detail and sightline at the fabrication plant, and witnessing a hose test for waterproofing. It was really fascinating to be so involved in the design and manufacturing process. Every day I kept the planning application documents and client presentation documents right there on my desk, which was a great insight into conveying your design ideas. There should be so much information you can find about your current project in the company files and documents. Ask your manager about them, which shows your appetite to fully understand the project.

My site experienced increased as well. Talking and reasoning with main contractors, suppliers, and consultants, whilst crucially understanding their position and preferences in relation to mine, was really eye opening. I made good professional friendships with them and was their first point of contact for day-to-day issues. Concerning our consultant 'design team' colleagues, I would often be told to give them a really hard time from the start of the project, and to put them on the back foot with their deliverables. My approach was that I want this consultant employee to produce their best work for me for the next few months or years, so I will start off positively by helping and encouraging them. They are far more likely to do what I need in that instance, than to be always nagging, bothering and disagreeing with them. Technically, you are the 'Lead Designer' and therefore must manage and coordinate with them. I wanted to make good contacts, be a positive person and see the results from that. You might witness that architects often have stereotypically negative views of what their consultants or suppliers will be like. Be aware that architecture professionals have certain reputations as well. It is all a bit tactical at times.

I think it is important to establish your own style in this regard. Everybody is a little bit different and everyone has a slightly different education and understanding of the industry. But you must be your own person, whilst taking influences from how other people work too. I would have loved a mentor at that time to push in certain directions and give advice. My director was a bit distant, not overly interested in my career or mentoring, but was always doing the best for the client and the project, so I learnt very high standards of project running from him. All that I really needed, was around 20 mins a week for an informal check in, someone to keep encouraging me and pointing out areas to improve. As it worked out, the mentoring time ended up most commonly being in the pub after work, or in casual chats with my architectural technologist peers.

Diving in

During several central London projects, the deadlines I experienced were tight, but realistic. I had great exposure to the fascinating relationship between client, architect and contractor. I attended and then chaired lots of meetings, usually with consultants, concerning coordination and design progress. The project size was ideal, because I was in touch with almost all project emails, and knew nearly everyone on the project. This gave me a lot of confidence about my role at the company, and each project was executed well on time and budget.

I took a bit of a risk once, after an office-wide email from the Managing Director concerning wages being frozen during the recession. It was just a year after the 2009 financial crisis, the company was generally doing well and getting lots of repeat business from trusted clients, and most jobs were being completed at profit. The problem was, this slightly negative email from the MD in mid-December, was sent just when everyone had been invited to the office kitchen point for some morning croissants and snacks. I decided, perhaps too forcibly, to dive in with a reply to the MD, pointing out the bad timing of communication and lack of positivity despite a tough year. I argued that just a small financial bonus for each staff member, like a couple of hundred pounds each to help Christmas costs, would be appropriate and very much deserved. I demonstrated with a few basic calculations in the email to back up my point. It was quite brave looking back, and potentially foolish, but it had a great response! Everyone in the company had a pay rise two months later. Fundamentally, I was speaking the truth and could back it up. But my opinion was made in an articulate, mature way, representing what I felt was quite a majority feeling within the company. We all know companies need financial safety and security, but small rewards go a long way at the right time.

Projects

My projects during these years were famous and historical parts of London. The brief was usually to reimagine the interior into premium office space. The final results were generally very similar, delivering gleaming white office spaces, featuring suspended ceilings and symmetrical grid layouts, with raised floors, very professional and impressive washrooms and then an entrance lobby design to give the corporate but artistic touch. They were different enough to take great lessons from each one. It was challenging when detailing around existing brick structures, or finding ways to maximize head heights despite restrictive beams, but it resulted in very inventive, original solutions. My best contribution was often pushing the design just to that extra little 5 or 10% to make it a really efficient floor space.

Daily tasks were coordinating with the consultants and keeping on top of all the outstanding design issues, to protect the designs we had first tendered. Attending meetings on-site or in company offices felt exciting and educational. I was being quite self-sufficient with enough on my plate, but with enough guidance from my project architects to ensure everything was staying on track and deadlines were being met. Back then, each drawing sheet was operating separately, in comparison to the BIM connectivity and software progression of today. But my attention to detail and strict organisation was well regarded, and allowed me to report back to my project architect with absolute certainty.

I still remember details I produced for those projects. I nearly made an artwork out of one just a few years ago. Whilst living in London, I would often check out the projects I had finished previously, so it was great seeing them occupied and my designs being there in the flesh. The company kept lining up great projects in interesting locations for me to dive into. I often coordinated the same drawing packages and all the cool looking designs of the entrance lobby and desk. The standard of detailing in this company was very rigid and consistent, so I always knew the sort of sharp, logical detailing that would impress my manager.

I was able to race through drawings and easily copy old details, demonstrating all the great effects you can get from simple shadow gaps, ceiling trims, skirting matching architraves, aligned tiling layouts, or corner details. These are the sorts of details that are easy to gloss over when you are in a well-designed space, but the more you get right down into the finer points, you realise that's the difference between nice designs, and really stunning architectural detailing. Rational proportions and pure alignment give that great sense of perfection. My manager would always say 'the devil is in the detail', meaning you would need to get deep into sketching, modelling and testing some options, in order to find the best design outcome.

Early ambitions

I was soon hitting a peak at this company after seven years, and was starting to wonder what projects I wanted to do for the rest of my career. I was branching out to bigger ideas and had always wanted to work on sports stadiums. I had really enjoyed what I had done so far, and could have carved out a really specific and valued niche for myself at that company, but my attitude was 'work to live', instead of 'live to work'. There are so many career opportunities, that I realised I wanted to break free and experience the wider world. The loyal and committed attitude that some people have to one company for many years is extremely commendable, but I was looking for variety, exciting projects and international travel. Knowing which side of this fence you sit on is perhaps the difficulty.

3.5 BREAKAWAY MOVE

- ▫ A big jump
- ▫ The dream
- ▫ The nightmare
- ▫ Back on the wheel

A big jump

Not many colleagues had ever talked about working abroad. Many European countries were represented in the London office, and I considered myself to be in one of the most prime architectural locations already. Perhaps because my recent projects were all quite small and similar, this had pushed me towards considering a new start and to branch out. I had lots of commercial, historical renovations under my belt now, but not a variety of typologies. Travelling so much around Europe for weekend holidays trips had really opened up my understanding and appreciation of buildings in major European cities. London is a pretty spectacular place, but stimulating and impressive styles are possibly stronger in cities like Berlin, Paris, Copenhagen, Amsterdam, Rome or Prague. Their ornate and historical gems are complimented by vibrant, modern equivalents. There are always things to be learnt from travel.

It was a sporting occasion that pushed me to break away from all that London had to offer. England had qualified for the 2014 World Cup in Brazil, and sports stadiums had always been a huge passion in my personal and professional life. I love the amazing theatrical typology of sports architecture, which really capture the sporting moments we keep so close to heart. This typology of architecture can mold a moment so vividly, because you can picture the exact surroundings and events of the day so many years later.

I had often read about globally influential companies completing major projects and stunning sized schemes, but I never thought I would be involved. Massive projects like airports and stadiums just need more people than normal projects, and the regular people like me still arrange drawings or coordinate design. So, it was my intention to travel to Brazil, watch some of the World Cup and find work on the Olympics building. Rarely do plans end up exactly as intended, but I wanted to break out from the cycle of the past six or seven years and do something wild. If it all went wrong and I came back to London, then I would have to take that on the chin and move on. It would be worse if I had stayed, knowing that I wasted a good opportunity.

The dream

I made endless LinkedIn connections, searched agency sites, contacted recruitment companies, and took advice from anywhere to understand the building programme for the Olympics. It was a bold choice, but an individual and calculated move.

So, the CV writing began again, whilst building up my portfolio and arranging cover letters or introductory emails about myself. A quick tip here is, to always keep hard copies or multiple pdf files of your previous work. There might come a time when you really need examples to hand. Whether sketches, drawings, photos or models, they will be great to look back on, and invaluable in potential job searches. I had kept a variety of documents from nearly all previous projects, so that soon enough I had the full four items going along in unison (CV, portfolio, website, and LinkedIn profile). My CV was informative, making a priority of showing my roles held and real project experience gained.

After arriving in Rio de Janeiro and finding my rented accommodation, I would spend several hours a day learning Portuguese and arranging whatever I could find for interviews or connections for the Olympics building. There were lots of warnings of corruption, and I truly got used to the 'maybe/no/yes' attitude from people in the industry. Eventually a project managing employee messaged back and said I could meet him for an interview at the official Olympics Committee head office. I had a great interview with him, meeting many different people in the office. For such a massive building project, there was so much to find out. The design had mostly been done months ago by international companies, and the on-site building regulations were always going to be quite a lottery in Brazil. But the challenge here was for the Olympic Committee or local companies to find people who can execute the job, cheaply and quickly. Gradually it all seemed a bit unclear who the decision makers were. Eventually having lost my passport, wallet and money to thieves, something was telling me it was not going to work out. A committee contact then officially told me that the international recruits had been finalised for this particular year, so I would have to wait five months for a new intake of Olympics employees. It all became a bit shady.

The nightmare

When disappointment hits, I think what is important is your reaction. Positivity about what you are aiming for next shows character and dedication to strive. You still have to improve yourself and build up enough experience in order to bounce back from negatives. The lesson to take forward when speaking to anyone in the industry, is that everyone has had a tough time. The natural human reaction when someone tells you of their recent bad luck, is to focus on how it's going to improve, or tell them they will be ok. I had to put this behind me and move on, knowing there is always another chance around the corner.

Back on the wheel

So, the Olympic dream was dashed, and I was back in the UK again, selling myself through emails and professional connections. Particularly via a friend's contacts in Abu Dhabi, I was trying to absorb all that was happening in the Middle East region. It seemed like an exciting and very different place to be. Many well-known companies had presence in the Middle East, but the set up was quite different. It would not work in the same way as London or Europe. I visited for a week to gauge the job prospects, and after one formal interview with a small architect's practice, it became clear I would not be able to survive just as a CAD draughtsman. The market was not set up like I thought it would be. I would need to step up a level and be a team leader or consultant contact point, to give an extra layer of value. The set up in UAE is quite rigid in terms of who does what, and where your skills levels will be best placed.

Relevant experience really is the key bottom line. Prospective companies still need to know what job you can do for them, and how much it's going to cost them to do it. So, I quickly realised my angle in subsequent interviews, by talking up a leadership role, describing my experience on-site and how I could lead the technical side of the office, in addition to my standard software skills.

3.6 MIDDLE EAST ADVENTURE

- International step
- Global
- Probation extension
- Playground
- Temporary

International step

I enquired at the biggest architectural firm in the world, who were based in Abu Dhabi, via a LinkedIn contact in their Human Resources department. I wasn't sure if I would suit the company, but their hugely impressive portfolio around the world and recruitment drive in the Middle East made it a good choice. It would give my career and confidence a big boost to work for a company that had consistently been voted as the best. The options and opportunities that may come of this were particularly attractive, so balancing the usual priorities of commuting time, scope to grow in the company, projects on offer and overall wage level, all stacked up pretty well. I attended a great interview with a studio director where we had a good chemistry and she saw my enthusiasm. The whole office seemed very friendly and excited to have new starters, and it was great to meet the incredible mix of people in Middle Eastern commercial companies.

I had not paid enough attention to international architecture news over the years, despite the incredible high-rise skylines, futuristic projects and glitzy exteriors of Abu Dhabi and Dubai. Such a place just seemed beyond me. Maybe the day-to-day headlines and snippets of international lifestyle flashed past my eyes too many times and too quickly. Featuring the tallest building in the world from 2006, the Burj Khalifa, there were so many amazing hotels and resorts, ground breaking engineering challenges on the coastline, and a freedom of design not really experienced anywhere else. I learnt there was around 150,000 Brits living there when I moved, all working in the standard industries you would find in the UK, like finance, teaching, engineering, architecture, recruitment and hospitality. I now know places like Singapore, Hong Kong, Vietnam and Malaysia have some fascinating projects and a great expat lifestyle to offer as well. I hadn't opened my thoughts to this enough whilst my head was down in London, so if you ever get the chance, you really must view international work as a very privileged opportunity.

In the UAE, the stunningly ambitious designs and hefty budgets are a crazy example of what humans have done with the planet. There had been so much money to spend on development since the 1990s, that it perhaps lacked the more organic and natural growth to knit together streets and create interesting neighbourhoods. But the cities certainly made up for it with ground breaking architectural designs everywhere you look. In Dubai, I learnt to take a few seconds to really critique buildings, because the shapes and forms were mind bending. I would try to gauge what the strategy was in a design, what the key story was behind it, and what the driving force was for the concept. The UAE certainly has its fair share of odd looking, often empty, white elephant buildings, to go alongside the spectacular, imaginative designs, so it was a different kind of education to live there.

Hopefully you'll find some time to work abroad at some stage, although getting used to a new country is a strange thing to embrace. There is lots to adapt to and understand, which is both exciting and daunting. However, so many nationalities work around the world now, that you are never really far away from a familiar voice or accent and will always find interesting, kind people in the industry. Most of my new colleagues had gone through exactly the same process just weeks or months earlier, so I think the best lesson I learnt here was talking to people, being genuinely interested in their career story, and realising that listening can really load you up with plenty of good industry knowledge.

Being on the more technical side of project execution in Abu Dhabi meant that regulations, building styles and working practices were crucial for me to understand. By being positive and inquisitive to everyone, I received a lot of positive vibes in return about my career and where I had worked. It turned out that nobody in the office was particularly knowledgeable about the local building codes, because they act as an amalgamation of British and American equivalents. It was instantly a target for me to specialise in. I could put in a few hours extra study and be the main point of contact for this knowledge in the office.

Global

Quickly I saw that amusing balance of personalities

in the office as discussed previously. Who are the friendly people, who is stressed-out, who is the grumpy one, who is really positive, who is someone to look up to, and who might benefit from my expertise. My first project was a typically huge financial tower. In particular, I was working on the facade details, structural spans, slab details and interaction with the podium arrangement. It was a great package to start on, because I had plenty of past experience in that area, but the project lasted barely a few weeks before it was put on hold for financial reasons. An interesting way to start life in the Middle East, and a common pattern if you know the economy of the area.

There is a spectacular mix of cultures in the Middle East. And more commonly there are huge varieties of people thrown together in massive cities that are developing fast. It's a big challenge to live together in such a mixture, when we still feel fundamentally different in terms of the culture we come from and what we believe about the world. That instantly translates into a very democratic working atmosphere in UAE, where you have an incredible variety of opinions and skills in an office, which I really valued.

AutoCAD use was just being phased out in the office, and that meant more Revit usage. Before that happened, I specifically remember in the first two weeks of starting the job, being asked to draw a simple ramp section in AutoCAD and realising my skills had completely deserted me from a few years ago, I was not able to finish the task. That realisation was pretty stark. You might be at expert level on many things, but if a company needs X Y Z skills, and you have A B C, it doesn't matter, your skills are not needed. I think it is vital to stay aware of that and not be too blinkered in your capabilities.

What I liked about this office was a great design ethic, with plenty of internal concept competitions or design reviews, relying on the whole team contributing. The thoughts, opinions and conversation would flow, with quick freehand sketches pinned up everywhere, leading to different interpretations and interesting discussions. That lead to more ideas, more improvements, and I could gradually see how they all combine to unify the strongest themes from several different starting points. I learnt to speak up a bit more about my design style, especially at these open design reviews. I had some ideas, and felt I could talk about them openly because nearly every design would continually change anyway.

A slight turn for the worse came when I was drafted into an 'Architect of Record' role for a huge shopping centre, which was a pretty drab and functional experience, but still a learning experience. It was all about dates, deadlines, programmes and a never-ending list of acronyms. Checkpoints all relied upon other checkpoints. Various permits lead to other permits or certifications, and there was unfortunately zero design input. It appeared we were not doing anything other than attending meetings and reporting back some comments to our project managers. This was the furthest away from what I thought architect was all about. It was mostly like a secretary role. A few arguments over inclusions, omissions and variations kept things lively, but even a couple of site visits could not really make it very exciting. I absorbed the good, the bad and the confusing, all as an interesting experience and tried to understand why each company was making their demands. Everyone had their agenda, which in this instance was very clearly centered around money, but I was lucky to see it all first hand.

Probation extension

Then followed a few conceptual study projects for hotels and residences in Saudi Arabia and Kuwait. My 3-month probation period was also extended, because the experience so far in this company had lacked any continuity in terms of my contributions. My studio leader agreed that I had not really been in a position to show what I can do on live projects, especially with the shopping mall project being such a messy workload. I actually got an apology from three members of staff, saying they had never really introduced me to the project very well, and they hadn't had much time to help me settle in. I had asked them all for a more in-depth chat or to get out for lunch together, and even set out specific project questions in a long email. Unfortunately, it wasn't even answered for nearly three weeks.

Some offices can be very quiet at times, or quite boring and not very stimulating. Things nearly got a bit serious when on two particularly stressful days, I witnessed my project runner nearly have a meltdown very late into the evening, swearing, shouting and worrying about lines not printing on site sections. The sections were very basic and more diagrammatical, but my project runner seemed on the verge of a breakdown as we sat there deep into the night, once everyone else had gone home. I had a few bad night's sleep wondering how long the stress levels in the team would go on, but it's difficult to fit into every office and every project smoothly. It was quite an insight to see what the job does to people you are supposed to look up to, but it was a case of just getting through it, and persevering until the job was done.

Stress levels can get pretty high in the architectural world, but I was never going to lose my cool to the point of not being in control. Wherever you are working, it's just a job, you try your best every day, and be as positive as you can. But you will get another job one day, or maybe change careers, so treat it all as experience and enjoy the moment. There will be tough times that you need to be ready for, and expect. Getting to know your colleagues properly can never be underestimated, which was certainly lacking in this instance. The company could easily have let me go at this time, and my future would have become wildly different.

Playground

I was then asked to go to a theme park project, joining the site team for a huge new attraction being built in Dubai. There were not enough projects to keep everyone in the office, but this theme park scheme had a bad reputation for stressful, late nights. It would also be more than one hour drive away on a notoriously dangerous and fast main highway. The speed limit was 140kph but it seemed the minimum speed was about 139kph. A group of our staff were already stationed there, and a group of four more including me were picked out, but generally not keen to go. In this instance, my colleagues and I had quite a few questions and reservations about the costs of rental vehicles or petrol, and who would do the driving. One colleague was getting quite sensitive about their rights and when they would get home in the evenings, and if damage was caused to their car on the building site. My view was to take one of two options: complain, be awkward and disruptive in the face of your manager, or just try it to start with, be a positive reliable employee and it might actually work out well.

The project was on an airport-sized empty plot, and easily the biggest project I had ever worked on. The highlight was meeting and learning from infinite nationalities and personalities on the project. The combination and mixture of people was a daily surprise. Several of those close working relationships are still active now, and directly helped me secure future employment in Australia. Quick recommendations, or a glowing appraisal of you from past colleagues is definitely helpful. Employers always want someone who will be a good team member, so to have that in writing from others is invaluable, even if it just vouches for your attitude as opposed to your project output.

My daily tasks were mostly finishing or amending the construction details of 32 separate buildings on the theme park site. Some were the rides or virtual experiences; some were the coordination between the rollercoaster tracks and changeover sheds. Then back-of-house buildings typically needed correct drainage gradients, or roof levels clarified, or corner details being worked out. There were just so many drawings from the initial design, that hundreds of them were deliberately not complete to a buildable level, in keeping with contractual agreements. It was our job to fill those gaps, and to complete the design intent in the most efficient way without detracting or changing the appearance. The creative team were stationed in Los Angeles, and had made all the perfect 3D visual images. We had to try to stay as true to them as possible. It was a brilliant problem-solving exercise every day.

I walked round the site many times, chatting to all

manner of site workers, clients and consultants. One situation required drastic changes to levels and doorway ramps, so it was often a case of a chain-reaction impact from one design solution creating another problem. It was really up to me how I could present the problem and solution, by answering RFIs every day (Request For Information documents). It was genuinely enjoyable walking over to the Ghostbusters building, Hotel Transylvania or Smurfs village to assess the structural shells that had been built, and start to visualise the final details. The building standards were good, with correct membrane wrapping around structural elements and layering of finishing materials. The solutions I was drawing each day would probably be built by the next day, so it was pretty intense.

After nearly 18 months, the final few tasks before leaving the site were progressively getting less and less important. It was natural that the team would decrease, and billing rates meant my cost was being factored in to completing our deliverable, whilst holding a profit. It was quite a sad but inevitable day to be moving back to the office.

Remember that everything in the industry is a contribution to your experience, and therefore a positive step in your career. This was not an ideal project to work on, but, as I subsequently did in recent years, there's quite a skill to massaging your CV to make something sound better than it really was at the time. The language you use or the way in which you describe experiences can give a very good or bad impression. In this case, the experience initially seemed quite negative, but I jumped into it and loved the challenge of site work, and now it is one of my most treasured project memories, and everyone loves hearing about it. If you were employing someone, which side of their opinion would you like to hear? Someone that grabbed opportunities and tried to enjoy the chance, or someone who complained from the start and picked problems without suggesting any solutions?

Luckily there were some better project offerings now, like a massive Convention Centre in the desert, four mixed use towers in Dubai and a Media City concept design, where I was able to throw some imaginative ideas around and let loose with a bit more positivity and conviction than previously. I was adopted by the American offices in Charlotte and Denver for some remote work to help them through design stages, then also produced a concept study for a residential block in Mecca, Saudi Arabia. My favourite conceptual solution was for the Media City, and I would still like to roll it out one day if the right opportunity and brief comes along. I have got those drawings and ideas heavily guarded and in my head! I had enough experience in this region by now to know what I could do, know what level of presentation was expected, and be part of the educational experience of leading office design competitions.

Temporary

I had established a strong technical influence in this company, and was coordinating some initiatives like office mentoring, the design technology group, and staff social events. Looking back, I think I had earnt the trust of the managerial ranks, so that I could speak up if things were not being done very well. However, after what had been an amazing four and a half years in UAE, I had eventually decided to move on. Thanks to previous experience, I understood I was again just a temporary representative at this company, easily replaced, and should write a very thankful resignation letter. Quite often that is the essence of a job; you are doing a temporary job for mutual benefit. I was sure to take the positives and negatives together, and put the whole experience down as part of the overall journey. Is any job ever truly permanent?

3.7 TRAVELS TO A NEW START

- Targets
- Surprises
- The bigger picture
- Freedom

Targets

I took a few months break after leaving the UAE, filling time with some travelling experiences and some research into possible next moves. It was becoming clear that my wife's engineering company might offer her a role in Melbourne, so I once again began prepping my CV, but this time with a different visual angle on my experience. It's tempting to go back to the trusted CV layout and content, but this time I used a chart layout that visually demonstrated all my professional experience. I felt that experience was going to be most crucial for employers to see. I had communicated my profile and qualifications clearly too, but in terms of readability, I really liked this alternative option. It was clear, methodical, professional, and leaning toward the technical side of architecture.

Whilst waiting for the Melbourne move, I still need

some purpose and something to work on, so actually started penning this book. Aside from that, I looked into the Australian set up of building project execution, building regulations and current major projects. Specializing myself was more and more important, so I dived into facades, glazing and cladding research. Project wise, it was heritage projects and stadiums at the top of my list. Should I be a jack of all trades or master of just one? As long as your 'mastered' subject doesn't get diluted and superseded, it seems best to spread yourself to be flexible, but have a couple of particular specialisms.

It was a previous project contact from four years previously, who essentially got me a foot in the door with an architectural firm in Melbourne that I had admired for many years. I think in the architecture industry, you are only ever about two or three steps away from nearly anyone in terms of contacts and links. This was an ideal way to get to the front of the queue, having an ex-colleague saying they had worked directly with me directly and could support my application. In reality, the biggest architects' firms are receiving several hundred CVs and portfolios every week, so just sending them out blindly to all companies is probably a bit too generic.

Surprises

After a few weeks researching, I had two offers from Melbourne companies and, after a couple of days consideration, I went for the company that I had admired for years. It was a close call, but I slept on it, used the points rating system discussed earlier, went with my gut instinct and confirmed for sure the next day.

It was a funky studio office over three levels, with

a workshop and timber interior vibe, but the project I ended up working on was disappointingly poor. It featured a painfully strange cladding design, an awful material combination, and a core located tight to the building edge. There was no daily leadership in terms of design experience, intent, or strategy. I thought the team needed that mentor figure and someone who was driving the design each day, and to be honest I was really keen to be that person. I was placed into the standard Revit-monkey role, and it soon seemed to me that lots of staff were quite underused and undervalued.

You never quite know what companies are like in reality, when you think from years of reading about them that they'll be a superbly run company with thriving employees. Plenty of team members were not that happy and just quite bored with what should be such a great job. It was a strange atmosphere and decreased my motivation in terms of development.

The bigger picture

I requested some direct chats with my director, and was surprised to hear "sorry I'm too busy" from him. There was nothing to suggest I could trust my director, and I did not feel like he would trust me. I think the decision had already been made to let me go after six months of probation. And when that happened it was quite a relief. Another learning experience to look back on.

It has seemed to me that big companies are mostly relying on their leading reputation to attract lots of staff, but don't need to put much effort into those newer employees until quite a few years of service. This is a very crucial point to know, when taking your own employment choices. Benefits of a smaller team or company who are more engaged in your development can be a big driver in your informative years, so take some time to research what your best move is, dependent on where you are in your career and what the priorities are.

In the bigger picture of my career path, it is great to have big name companies on my CV, but each job is another little part of your overall journey. I think you can afford a couple of sidesteps or diagonal career steps, because every move is unlikely to be a perfect step forward each time. The biggest concern is whether they fit with your personal aspirations and core values. Feeling undervalued or unchallenged was quite a big problem for me, so it shows you still need drive and meaning in your everyday work.

Freedom

So, I found myself with a few weeks off, and was immediately thinking ahead to the next exciting step. There was suddenly a huge range of possibilities for where I could turn to next. Could I go straight into another similar role in a smaller company, or hold off and realign my career? Just from a few hours brainstorming, I wondered what I could do to improve myself. Retraining in the industry? How to be a bricklayer, tradesperson or site manager? Maybe follow up an old contact through CIAT in specification writing? Otherwise, undertake some new qualifications in sustainability or similar. I even considered a government policy or authority job in architecture or the built environment. My driver was a capacity to keep learning and keep improving. Many people in the industry have had many serious setbacks over recent years, but I realised it is often how you describe your career that can give the experience a whole new feeling. Whatever nightmares you've had, try speaking about them as valuable, exciting development steps, and you might feel very differently about what you can offer going forward.

Particularly this year and last, many people were confronted with life changing and financially damaging changes from the Coronavirus pandemic that could define their years ahead. You have to remain positive and take the lessons in life forward, and leave the rest behind only as memories.

3.8 DIAGONAL STEP

- ▫ Opportunities
- ▫ A new direction
- ▫ Adapting
- ▫ The path ahead

Opportunities

My first specification experience came years ago, when our in-house spec writer was completely overloaded with deadlines. A company decision was made to let 'normal' staff (like me) jump into the software and create their own specifications. At the time it was very difficult to find qualified staff to undertake such a risky part of the business, but it was seen as a good step to educate from within. I put my hand up to give it a go. It wasn't an easy transition, but with some good grounding and logically working through the same structure of information in the specification, it became an extra skill that I could talk about.

A colleague from CIAT had relocated to Australia several years ago, and had been setting up the reams of specification content before it would be rolled out across the Australian market. The timing of my message was ideal because the company was just going live with specification writing software and model integration. The blend between software companies and architects is a strange one because typically you are mixing IT and sales people with architects, who can be vastly different on how they like things done. However, I was an ideal fit to bridge that gap with my Revit skills, and give real industry insights.

As mentioned previously, keeping contacts and having plenty of ex-colleagues 'in the back pocket' should always come in handy. Once an initial discussion took place, taking a job with the specification writing platform was always going to fit really well with my overall career pattern, future plan and professional development. I was aware of the company many years ago in the UK, but would never have looked upon it as a career choice back then. Although saying that, I always knew a career based on technical, building and product knowledge would be suitable for me. I didn't really want to get into another company, only to become a victim of the pandemic issues and perhaps leave again three months later. In keeping with my own advice, I slept on it for a couple of days and confirmed it was a great opportunity with very progressive goals and targets in mind for me, which would contribute to whichever direction my career would take in future.

A new direction

My CV showed the right skills for what the company were trying to expand with, so after a 30 minutes chat about the company direction, gauging what I can bring to the team, it was fairly clear this would be a good option.

There are masses of software on the market now for all areas of architecture and project execution. Some of them seem invaluable whereas as some seem far too complicated. But there was a great start-up attitude in this company, and therefore the scope to make the role what I wanted it to be, trying to build various industry strategies and revenue streams for this intuitive specification platform. The company trusted my judgment and realised my architecture experience gave a good insight. I really felt the trust from my mangers and with the work from home transition (I didn't meet my colleagues in person for nearly seven months), there was lots of opportunity to research and consider future developments. As I've thought many times, life is a long journey, and your career is a long and winding road, so you can make some slightly diagonally moves when it feels right.

I hadn't given much appreciation for the man hours required to compile all that clause content for specifications behind the scenes. It was a good start to understand the depths of architectural small print, away from the comparatively easy task of modelling and creating drawings. Once you've read a specification fully, or seen how a main contractor has to deal with it, it really does come down to nuts, bolts and fixings to put these amazing buildings together. I think once you know the science and technology behind a building, your understanding and confidence will sky rocket.

As far as my career experience has taught me, there has not been much development of specifications and the way they are applied until quite recently. A big step has finally arrived by combining the power of embedded (and often lost) model information directly with writing the specification at the same time. Up until now they have been very separated, which is totally flawed in this age of connected thinking and technology. In years to come, I think the online models will be automatically writing the specification for you, depending on what products you pick from BIM objects and components. Compiling a specification in the background shouldn't be that hard, because for the vast majority of works packages, you don't need innovation, you actually need certainty, reliability, consistency and simplicity.

Adapting

Specifications had forever been a huge A4 printed document in my career. But specifications are rarely printed in full now, because huge PDF documents can be scrolled through and navigated easily on screen. Only the necessary specification information should be shown and linked where needed, so the process has improved from the previous detachment. I think current and future connectivity will allow only the relevant clauses to show up at exactly the relevant places, with more individual liability to each manufacturer and installer. The specification document can be and should be pretty simple. In fact, it works better to stay very clear and concise. I certainly look forward to those technological improvements like model connectivity, making everyone's job easier, in terms of the expanding bureaucracy and regulations that are crunching the design process. The specification should complement the design and project process, not restrict it.

Stereotypically, and in reality in my career,

specification writers were the quiet, older guy in the corner of the office, not really speaking to anyone because, in truth, the world of specs can be a little tedious. However, because this is changing, it is beneficial to have a go yourself if the opportunity arises, and prove you can put your hand to anything in the industry. An architecture professional below 30 years of age who is involved in specifications is very rare and valuable thing. After all, specifications are just the written form of project, so the knowledge is usually already there.

In practice working with specifications, I still enjoy going to product websites to see how companies are presenting their products. Sustainability aspects, raw materials and relevant standards are common questions the specifier is going to ask, so to show that information clearly up front is important. Being able to describe nearly everything about how the project works and the science behind it, in order to feel like the most intelligent person on the project, was the sort of mantra that kept me going. (often not the case admittedly, but it gives you a big confidence boost).

The path ahead

Finding time to investigate building products and understand changes in the market, that I wouldn't usually see from the blinkered view of project deadlines, was a refreshing change to project work. I am currently learning a huge amount about the background fabrication for architectural products, and where all those materials come from. The implementation of specification documents within Revit and ArchiCAD models means there is a different aspect of the project documentation I am having to work with. These are the skills needed for my job at this particular time. They weren't useful skills at the start of my career and may again become obsolete in ten years time. It's that same ongoing challenge to keep learning, keep your skills relevant, and enjoy all that the industry has to offer.

Just a few years ago I didn't have much in depth knowledge of specifications. It was a part of the industry that many professionals may never truly get their head around. Adaptability is crucial to your development because as hopefully shown in the previous sections of this book, there is so much to learn in the industry that you never know which area you might be thrust into next. But being able to tackle it with some degree of confidence and slowly educate yourself into a position of expertise will be making a continual positive contribution to your career path.

SECTION 4 – SUMMARY

You've probably noticed the running theme in this book. Architecture will not be the same in just a few years' time, so adaptation is all part of your career. But so is enjoyment, fulfilment and betterment of yourself and your life.

For me, starting out in architecture as an absolute novice in the late 90s, going through four mixed years at university, coming out into the world of work in 2005, leaving London in 2013 for a failed dream, and now landing in Australia in 2020 (at least for a few years) means that I have seen first-hand, how the industry is hugely unpredictable but incredibly enjoyable.

I've readied myself for that change, and always like to take a little look ahead and wonder what might happen next. Maybe skillsets will change, design will evolve, materials will be invented, software will improve, and professionals will need to be useful in different ways to get buildings built. Nearly everything in the industry could change.

My career has not panned out the way I first thought it would. To be honest, at 22 years old after my university degree, I was not thinking about my plans that seriously. I thought I could just be comfortable working on a variety of projects and buildings for the rest of my career and keep it all very consistent. But after a few years understanding broadly what it's all about, I started to appreciate and desire a bit more control over how to manage my own way forward. I didn't want to just coast between a few different projects on whatever was put in front of me. I wanted to experience some specific roles, specific typologies, and of course different countries.

I still have various aspirations and interests going forward, both professionally and personally. For example, every young architecture professional wants to design their own house, don't they? It really is your life the way you want to run it. Jobs will come and go, projects will come and go, and you will have a few knockbacks to go with your big achievements. Your plan might be rigid and specific, with companies, projects or locations clearly identified. Or you might want to go with the flow and see what crops up. It's impossible to plan out your career, but perhaps a rewarding career would be impossible without a little bit of planning. Work is just one part of your life, so your professional plan should also fit in with who you are, what you want to do, and the bottom line of what is going to make you happy in life. There is nothing worse than meeting someone who hates their job, which effects their life and happiness, but they don't seem to be doing anything about it.

This book was written primarily as an advice resource for young architecture and design professionals. I hope it has given you many good points of view, a few interesting angles on real life situations, and a bit of industry information that might not otherwise be covered when you first jump into employment. Everything is a learning process, because aside from being a huge subject, so much is changing and improving. There are new things constantly adding to that spectrum of information.

I think this is a hugely exciting but hugely challenging time to be involved in architecture, with so many ways in which you can offer your skills. Clients and developers are generally pretty sharp with their investments now, looking at many innovative, groundbreaking and intelligent building results, but in return wanting to know and guarantee that it's going to be effective. The architecture industry still has to be one step ahead of that, to know how it can be done, and how people can more effectively use buildings. That is still the main skill that you possess; a knowledge of how we design, construct, and use buildings.

I said earlier; architecture represents democracy to me. It can represent all sorts of other things as well, but knowing that famous architects of today started off as young, excited students and eventually designed a building that we might globally know and love, shows that architecture is something you can jump into and devote yourself to, from scratch. From the biggest and best-known buildings to the smallest local private projects, you are making a contribution to the places that we all share.

The world of architecture in its fundamental principle is to build, and therefore to add something, and therefore to contribute. It should be an industry and job that leaves you positive and optimistic about what you are creating.

ABOUT THE AUTHOR

Joseph is a chartered architectural technologist from
Milton Keynes in the UK.
After initially studying Architecture Part 1 at Nottingham
University in 2001, Joseph left with a BA (Hons) degree in
Architectural Studies in 2005.
16 years, 3 continents and 7 companies later in the industry,
Joseph decided to write down his experiences and thoughts
about dealing with the early years of employment, and how
young architecture professionals can forge a strong and
rewarding career path ahead.
Joseph currently lives in Melbourne, Australia, and works in
architectural specifications.

Printed in Great Britain
by Amazon